ONE GRAND ADVENTURE

JACK PENROD

Fedd Books
P.O. Box 341973
Austin, TX 78734

www.thefeddagency.com

Published in association with The Fedd Agency, Inc., a literary agency.

ISBN: 978-1-957616-33-9
eISBN: 978-1-957616-34-6

LCCN: 2023900444

Cover design by Mackenna Cotten
Printed in the United States of America

For my children, my beautiful wife Lucia, and all the friends and family who lived the journey with me. Thank you for being a part of my grand adventure.

TABLE OF CONTENTS

FOREWORD

A few years back, I came across a book titled "I Married Adventure." The title struck a chord in me. It felt as if it was speaking to me. After looking through the pages, I realized its stories were about actual travel adventures. But what a title for me! It totally described my life with Jack.

When you first meet Jack, you cannot help but feel his immense inner power, his calming demeanor, and his friendly face. You are immediately drawn to him, wanting to get to know him better. As you can imagine, I am speaking from my own experience and I promise, I'm not being biased. I also see the reaction of everybody else when they first meet him. What a nice guy!

As his assistant for many years, I watched as Jack treated everyone he met with respect and consideration, never losing his temper or control. I also noticed how people were always trying to please him. When Jack was disappointed in someone's performance, boy... disappointment was somehow worse than anger or yelling. Their reaction was as if they'd been punched in the face! No one wanted to let him down. It was amazing to watch and my curiosity took over.

As I learned more about his past, my curiosity spiked even higher. His childhood was full of tragedy and trauma, but also of perseverance and overcoming the challenges thrown at him. Raised with three other siblings by a single, teenage mom in extreme poverty and receiving no college education, Jack had built himself into a powerful force. Who wouldn't be curious? What kind of courage does it take for a little boy to decide that survival was not enough, it would not be his only goal? How can a person come from this background and bring themselves to living a life at a level known only to a few? At times, I wished I could live inside his brain for a few weeks to see how it works!

Another thing that struck me about Jack was his humbleness. I've known many successful people with humble beginnings that disconnect from their past to create a new story and leave their families behind. Jack was never like this. He was so proud and loving with his mom and siblings. He was proud to introduce them to all his fancy and wealthy friends and I loved that about him. Married three times (the third time's the charm—me!), we have a blended family and his kids are, like he says in his book, his biggest adventure. Regardless of where he was in life, he stayed as close as he could to be available to them always. He adores them.

Being married to Jack for 27 years has definitely not been boring. I don't know where he gets so much energy! We have a big age difference but I have to tell you, sometimes I cannot keep up. Out of everyone I've ever known, Jack puts them all to shame. He's the best free diver, the best golfer, the best tennis player, the best card player, and on and on. My friends used to say that he was like Dorian Gray sucking their energy and they were becoming older than Jack! It helped that I was younger than him, naive about all the possible dangers that come with his adventures. After years of being part of quite a few of those adventures, I started calling him Indiana Jones. You see, he never thought twice about taking chances. If he didn't come back with cuts and bruises, he didn't have a good time. Then, you see him at work and he has the same calmness and chilled zen-like attitude that puts everyone at ease.

All of us know the famous phrase "The American Dream". For people like me who were born outside the United States, this meant that with hard work you can achieve your wildest dreams. In reality though, it's not that simple! But Jack makes it look easy. There's something about Jack that makes him an extraordinary man.

The project of writing his biography was a long process. When I first told him, why don't you write a book? His response was NO! What's so special about it? Who would want to read it?

It was my turn to sell to the master salesman. Why was it so hard for him to see himself the way we all do? His story is inspiring and funny, filled with beautiful, happy moments but also hardships. His story is full of life lessons and adventures others will only dream of. I asked him to do it for our twins, his youngest kids, Isabella and Jake, who came into Jack's life when he was in his 60's. There is so much the kids would never know about their dad, and I wanted them to be as proud of Jack as I am. Proud of the extraordinary man that is their dad. So, the project started.

Once he started writing the book and I was privileged to read the drafts, I have to tell you, I couldn't put it down!!! Stories that I'd never heard and the ones I'd gotten to be a part of, all new, fresh, and captivating in Jack's own words. Reading this book also gave me the privilege of knowing Jack more profoundly than ever before. As Jack wrote, the book turned from a family heirloom into a story that needed to be shared with the world. You're gonna laugh, you're gonna cry, but mostly you'll be inspired.

I feel so lucky and blessed to be part of his life, his story, and his adventures. He has enough material to write a couple more books, believe me, but for now, we invite you to step into his life and learn from a simple man that knew what he wanted and worked hard for it every day.

Lucia Penrod
Wife, Mother and CEO

THE LONG WAY HOME 01

"A good parent prepares his children. You can't force your family into anything,
but you can show them the way that they will most likely succeed and be happy."

—JACK

In 1956, I went spearfishing behind Miami's Deering Estate and got my nose cut off. Believe it or not, a spear had nothing to do with it.

I had been swimming in shallow water, scanning the sand for fish. When I came up from the bottom, a Portuguese man-of-war was attached to my back. If you're not familiar with the man-of-war, it's a scarier jellyfish with stinging, venom-filled tentacles.

The pain was so excruciating that I dove back in, trying to get him off of me. In my momentary panic, I smashed my face against a rock. Because my mask was glass, it shattered, cutting a deep gash into my face.

Luckily, I was diving with a friend. He had a car nearby, and he drove me to the doctor. The blood was profuse. The nurse who walked in was actually a friend of mine. She took one look at me and

1

fainted. I realized then that my nose had been nearly severed, dangling on the right side of my face. The doctors stitched me up, and it was no big deal. It did leave a pretty big scar.

Later in life, I met a doctor who worked on scar removal. The scar had never really bothered me, but he seemed excited to work on it. So I drove to his practice in Ohio where he took some kind of an electrical wire brush to my nose. The next thing I knew, I was covered in blood. But the scar was gone. The brush all but flattened it out—hardly noticeable now, even to me.

The thing about scars is that every one of them comes with a story. And let me tell you, I've got plenty of both—scars *and* stories. I've had a life filled with adventures.

I've been poor, and I've been rich. Both more than once.

I've flown planes . . . and had a few close calls.

I've started businesses on various continents.

I've dropped myself into primitive habitats to live off the land alone.

I've met A-list celebrities and hosted them at my beach clubs.

I've thrown parties so big that an entire city asked me to scale down my marketing efforts.

I've done a lot of things and been a lot of places, but the most remarkable experiences I've had have been with my family. I really mean that.

People will ask me, "Jack, how'd you make it so far in business and still have good relationships with your family?"

There's not a direct answer to that question. Instead, there are a series of answers. Stories, really, that I hope express how fortunate I feel to have been successful in both business and in family. Maybe I've just been lucky. Maybe I've created my own luck. I suspect it's probably a little bit of both.

What I can tell you for certain is that it has required hard work, self-belief, and positivity.

And that it's all been worth it.

If you like adventure stories, my life is full of them. Join me as I share some highlights *and* low points of my family, business, and life.

* * *

I never turned in one assignment when I was in high school.

All I knew were sports. I was the best track star in the state: I never lost a single event—not the 100 meters, the 200 meters, the shot put, or the discus. I weighed 180 pounds at five-foot-nine. I played halfback on our football team too. I still held records at my school up until a few years ago. I guess the teachers just passed me from one grade to the next so I could compete, because I graduated without ever having read a single book.

It wasn't until I joined the Marine Corps right out of high school that I realized I had some brain along with my brawn. And my brain wasn't all that bad.

All 400 soldiers in my recruitment class took the ASVAB—a military aptitude test. For the most part, the ASVAB is an evaluation of your ability to solve problems.

The colonel called me into his office. I thought for sure they were going to kick me out because I'd failed it so miserably.

"Out of 400 applicants," he said, getting right down to business, "you got second."

Second? I thought surely there'd been a mistake, but I certainly wasn't going to point it out. Turns out I scored a 140 on the test. The average Marine doesn't approach 100.

Before I knew it, they were begging me to be a pilot. "Will you sign up?" they asked. "We'll pay for everything."

I said, "Wait a minute. Why are you chasing me?"

I had already been playing golf with the colonel—giving him lessons, really—and I knew he didn't give a dang about the military. One of the unexplainable themes of my life has been that every time I walk into a room, I'm put in charge of something. I walked into my barracks along with 70-plus other Marines. The sergeants looked at me and said, "You're in charge," and left.

I don't want to pretend at anything, but I think I've always had this quiet confidence that puts people at ease. That's what my wife, Lucia, tells me anyway.

Growing up, I had no idea I was capable of becoming a pilot for the Marines. But I did know how to earn a living. I got my first job when I was six years old. Actually, I had three jobs. I had a paper route, I sold Coca-Colas at the Ohio State stadium, and I cleaned bakery pans for the local prison. Not long ago, I got a statement from the Social Security administration that told me I made $1,500 that year—in 1945. That's close to $25,000 by today's standards. Not too bad for a first-grader on welfare.

My parents were poor. The first years of my life were the final years of the Great Depression—or, at least, that's what the history books say. In Columbus, Ohio, the Depression lasted a lot longer for my family than it did for many others. I had two brothers and a sister, and there was never enough space or money.

It wasn't that we couldn't afford the newest action figure or luxury sedan in our home—we barely had enough money for basic needs like food, shelter, and clothes. The financial strain weighed heavily on my parents, and tensions were constantly high.

Looking back, I now understand that my parents were children themselves who were trying to raise a big, young family during extremely difficult times. My mother, Ruth, was just 16 when she met my father. She was beautiful. People used to say she looked like a movie star. She turned a lot of heads. My father, Chester, was a handsome guy too. When the playhouse came to town, they asked him to be a stand-in for Clark Gable. He had an easy charm about him—charisma.

My parents had a lot going for them. They looked every bit the wholesome, attractive 1930s teenage couple. Until my mother got pregnant.

A teenage pregnancy would have been difficult in any era, but it was especially scandalous in the American heartland during the years before World War II. Everyone in the family had an opinion about how the shocking development should be handled. My grandmother was a devout woman whom everyone called "Grandma Townsend." Despite being a kind lady, Grandma Townsend had a strict edge to her, borne out of her strong sense of right and wrong.

She had adopted my mother and expected a certain standard from her—a standard that did not include her getting "in trouble" as a sophomore in high school. In July 1938, my mom delivered my older brother, Chuck. Both sets of their parents were so upset with my mom and dad that they refused to let them live with them.

"But," my father's mom, Grandma Penrod, told them, "you can stay in the chicken coop behind the house."

With nowhere else to go, Mother, Dad, and Chuck spent that first year living in a newspaper-lined chicken coop.

Just two months after Chuck was born, Mother was pregnant again. I arrived on June 25, 1939—a month before Chuck's first birthday. By then, Chuck had softened Grandma Townsend's stance against my parents' relationship. My parents had gotten married before I was born, so the family now had access to her home—a remarkable improvement over the chicken coop.

I was born in an upstairs bedroom with the help of a midwife. After my birth, Grandma Townsend allowed us to move into a duplex she owned near her house. We would live in one side, and she would rent out the other. I lived the first years of my life in those modest surroundings. But I didn't know any different. It was home. It was also how I got the gig cleaning bakery pans.

The renter who leased the other side of the duplex was the prison baker. He approached me one day and said, "I could use some help cleaning the sheet pans. You want to make some money?" So we'd use this special entrance to the jail, and once the food was served, I'd scrape down the pans and oil them up for the next round.

I didn't really understand why my parents didn't get along. For one thing, I was very young. For another, I didn't really get to know my father. He was often distant and unapproachable, unlike my mother, who was warm and loving. It wasn't until I was an adult that I learned about my father's shortcomings—and how they affected my mother.

My father worked hard, but the bulk of the family responsibility fell on my mother. In addition to running the home and taking care of two young babies, she also had to find a way to make ends meet. My father worked nights on the railroad—long, dirty hours of manual labor that often left him too tired to play with us when he got home. He was not too tired, however, to see other women. He would sometimes bring the other girls by the house in full view of us kids. His brazenness infuriated my mother. Their fighting intensified. It wasn't just that he was running around on her; it was that he had no problem rubbing it in her face.

Women found my father irresistible. He often spent money he didn't have to show these girls a good time. He felt no shame in his actions. And if he ever did have any remorse about the way his actions hurt Mother, he never showed it.

But Mother's top priority wasn't Dad. She focused all of her energy on providing for her children. Each morning, she would put on a nice dress and head downtown to work as a sales clerk at Lazarus department store, a midwestern retail chain that eventually merged with Macy's. She was on her feet all day. It was the first in a long line of jobs I remember her having. She was willing to do whatever it took to take care of us. After long days working on the sales floor, she would be exhausted when she finally got home.

Despite the bad blood between my parents, our family continued to grow. My sister, Carol Ann, was born in 1945. My little brother, Bob, came along in 1947. We were now a family of six, but we still were barely making ends meet. In nearly every picture from this time period, us kids were wearing secondhand or donated clothes—pea coats from the Salvation Army, hand-me-downs from other children. Despite our threadbare appearance, I never felt poor. I just felt like my life was a big adventure.

Mother meticulously watched every penny. We lived off coupons, buying war-rationed items whenever they were available. By the time I was seven or eight, one of my regular jobs was to pick up the groceries. If Mother gave me a grocery list and $1.37 to take to the store, the items on the list would total $1.37 to the penny. I'm sure it took Mother a lot of time and effort for her to plan out our meals, but her painstaking preparation kept us afloat.

In the mid 1940s, a dollar could go a long way. Milk was a nickel per quart, and flour was a quarter for a five-pound bag. While our meals were never fancy, we never went to bed hungry.

While my parents worked, the kids would spend our time at Grandma Townsend's house. Although she was a strong woman, she was never harsh with us. She adored us and treated us well, letting us do things she would never have allowed her own children to do. Grandpa Townsend was a kind, good-natured man too. He spent a good deal of time playing with us. One of my earliest memories is sitting on his lap and spiking his hair straight into the air.

We didn't grow up with a lot of toys, but my grandparents had a midwestern sensibility that helped them come up with things for us to do. They had an old-fashioned washtub in the basement that we used to wash our clothes by hand. During the winter, we would use the tub for its primary purpose and hang the wet clothes up in the basement. In the summers, though, Grandpa Townsend would drag the tub upstairs to the backyard and we would take turns using it as a swimming pool. They wanted us to be happy.

And generally we were happy. But life wasn't easy. One of the worst things about poverty is that it separates children from their parents at an early age. Mother wanted to spend time with her growing family, but she was overwhelmed with the responsibilities of providing for us. We frequently ran around unsupervised—a side effect of having two parents who worked long hours. It's not that we were neglected. Mother loved us deeply and worked to make a better life for us all.

Despite being poor—or maybe because of it—I quickly grew to understand the importance of hard work. That's how I came to work three jobs before the ripe old age of seven. But it didn't feel like a burden, and my parents never asked me to help out. I wanted to. Plus, work was fun. I had experiences I would never have had otherwise. I got to see much more of the world than other kids my age. For me, work was and has always been exciting.

Although making money was always a priority, I also understood the necessity of having fun. I probably got that trait from my dad. He worked hard and played hard, which is something I have always valued, even if I don't approve of some of the play my dad indulged in. I continued to seek adventure.

When I was nine, the newspaper I worked for held a contest to see which of its carriers could sell the most newspapers. Game on. I went door to door, knocking and pitching papers to homeowners. I had no idea how I'd stack up against the competition, but I knew they wouldn't beat me in effort. Sure enough, at the end of the contest, I was the winner.

The prize was a trip to the Indianapolis 500. I boarded a train all by myself and headed from Columbus to the Indianapolis Speedway. Today's adults would never dream of allowing their kid to do that, but when I asked my mother, she said, "Okay. Go on." I'd been working jobs for three years by then, and I think she sensed I was responsible enough to get there and back safely. The next year, I won a trip to a Cleveland football game. There was another train ride, another adventure. The travel was as exciting as the game itself. The freedom, the experiences—they were intoxicating.

But all was not well at home. The years of backbreaking work on the railroad had taken their toll on my father's health. He was losing his hearing from the loud atmosphere of the railroad, and he was constantly tired. Though still a young man in his 20s, he was starting to move like he was much older. In 1949, when I was ten years old, he borrowed $1,000 from Grandma Townsend to start an automobile body shop . He spent his time working on dented fenders and busted grills. I worked there with him sometimes, but he remained mostly distant and aloof.

By the time I was ten, I started delivering the *Columbus Dispatch*. It was 1949, and Ohio was not yet enforcing the federal requirements for work permits for minors. With nothing preventing me from getting a job, I loved the idea of a steady income.

I would show up early and collect the day's newspapers in a wooden box. Then I would sit in the distribution center and fold the papers before delivering them around the neighborhood. I tried to work as quickly and efficiently as possible. And that hard work was soon noticed. My bosses were impressed by my hustle and offered me new opportunities. Before long, I began doing two delivery routes a day—one in the morning, another in the afternoon

My parents never asked me to contribute to the family finances, but I did. With what was left over, I bought things I wanted and loaned money to my brothers—especially Chuck, who always seemed to be broke. I realized I could afford the things I wanted because I had worked hard for them. The lesson was not lost on me, and it would follow me for the rest of my life.

As the 1940s faded into the 1950s, my parents' relationship deteriorated even further. They yelled constantly. On a Friday in May of 1951, their constant bickering became violent for the first and only time. My father was caught in some sort of lie. He and my mother began arguing about his deceptions and infidelity. A tragic accident occurred, and my father died.

My life as I knew it changed forever. I wondered where we would live and who would take care of us. But mostly I wanted to be by Mother's side. I knew she must have been terrified and devastated.

My protective instincts kicked in. I was out delivering the paper when I got the news. I left my route to someone else and went straight home. That was the day I grew up and began taking responsibility for the well-being of my family. I would remain protective of Mother for the rest of her life.

With my father gone, everything felt different. The house was a constant reminder of that horrible day. Everywhere we went, Mother was subject to stares and whispers. As long as she stayed in Columbus, there would always be people who whispered. Among Mother's greatest critics were my father's relatives. Shortly after his passing, they came to the house and took everything that had ever belonged to him—clothes, books, even the photographs. They left us without a single memory of our father.

I never had a relationship with my father's family again—we were cut off. I also mourned the loss of the life I had once had. I knew that everything was going to be different and would never go back to the way it once was. Our financial problems would continue to get worse.

Tragedy has a way of bringing families closer, and we four kids became very protective of each other. During the summer and fall of 1951, we tried to rebuild the life we had. We muddled through each day in a daze. I returned to school and to my paper route, but everything was still different.

One day, a man came by the house and said he wanted to give us a car. He handed Mother the keys to a 1936 Oldsmobile, along with the advice to only drive it around town. But Mother had her own ideas. As the days grew shorter and nights grew colder, Mother came up with a plan to add some new sunshine to our lives.

One winter morning, she gathered us kids together and said, "If we're going to be poor, we will at least be warm." At some point she had decided to move us all to Florida—away from the judgmental eyes of Columbus, but also away from everything we had ever known. It must have been terrifying for her, but it was an exciting prospect to us kids.

My younger brother, Bob, was three or four at the time, and he ran around the house in cowboy boots. "I don't wanna leave!" he whined.

"But, Bob," Mother said, "we're moving to Texas!"

It was a lie, but Bob was happy and wouldn't know the difference anyway.

Everything about the Sunshine State seemed to be the land of our dreams—beaches, fishing, and new opportunities. So with little discussion—and a lot of excitement—we packed all of our earthly belongings into that beat-up Oldsmobile and headed south.

It was a five-day drive with five of us in the car. The man who gave us the Oldsmobile was right—it barely made the trip. It broke down multiple times during the journey, but we always got it fixed and back on the road. Despite the delays, we were all in good spirits. We knew better days were ahead.

Our new life was about to begin in South Florida—a place where I'd go on to create a family, many businesses, and a home.

HOMESTEAD

"Whenever someone asks me what I think of education, I always say it's very important. But if you can't afford a higher education, don't sit around saying 'woe is me.' Go get a job at a simple business. Learn some good work ethics and values. Learn how to fit into the community. Set some goals for yourself. If you learn those things, you've given yourself an education."

—JACK

To a ten-year-old, moving across the country is an adventure no matter what the circumstances. I felt like the move to Florida was a foray into the unknown—a chance for our family to start over with a clean slate.

It was wintertime in early 1952, and the idea of warmer weather and sandy beaches sounded like a dream. Everything back home was cold and dying. I remember watching the snow fall as we passed through Atlanta. Sitting in the back seat of the Oldsmobile, I watched the barren landscapes give way to the swaying palms of sunny Florida. With each mile, I was getting closer and closer to a whole new world.

After almost a week on the road, we finally arrived in Homestead, Florida. Despite our new location, some things hadn't changed. We were still poor, and now we didn't have my father's income to help support us. But I wasn't worried—we had always figured it out in Ohio, and I had no doubt we'd figure it out in Florida too.

We first settled in a migrant camp called the Hotel Redland. Built in 1904, the Redland was Homestead's first hotel, connected to a mercantile store, library, and post office. Today, the Redland is a trendy historic site that draws in tourists who want to see the remnants of old Florida.

But in 1952, the Redland was neither new nor historical. It was just a rundown boarding house full of farm workers and transients. I didn't mind it, but Mother thought the hotel was crowded, loud, and dangerous. She said it was no place to raise a young family. Using her considerable resourcefulness, she found a new place for us to live—an old doctor's office in nearby Kendall, Florida—a rural, unincorporated part of Dade County. With old jalousie windows and overgrown landscaping, the doctor's office wasn't luxurious, but it was clean and safe.

I don't know what Mother's agreement was with the landlord, but I imagine we lived there for free. We were probably responsible for the general maintenance and cleaning because we didn't have enough money to pay rent. The abandoned office was never meant to be a residential home, but we didn't mind. There were ample opportunities for adventure and fun. When we weren't working or in school, we could go fishing or exploring at the beach. The South Florida climate was agreeing with us.

If there was a silver lining in the tragedy that befell our family, it was in the sense of responsibility I quickly learned. I was comfortable taking the leadership role in the household. Hard work didn't bother me, and I enjoyed the feeling of satisfaction and independence it gave me. Even as a preteen, I recognized how hard my mother worked—how relentless she was in providing for all of us. More than anything, I wanted her life to be easy—or at least easier than it currently was. So, one day when I was twelve, I sat her down and made a solemn promise.

"Mother," I said, "I will be a millionaire someday, and you won't have to work. And when I'm a millionaire, I'll pay for our house."

She smiled at me warmly and said nothing at the time, although she would frequently remind me of that conversation. I don't know whether she believed I would become a millionaire or not, but it didn't really matter. What was important was that I believed me.

No one in our family ever thought manual labor was beneath us, so we all pitched in to fix up the old doctor's office and take care of the house. We also quickly got jobs. Since my mom was adopted, she didn't have many relatives. But she did have an adopted brother who worked at the Columbus Zoo and Aquarium. After she called him, he found jobs for us at a zoo in South Florida.

My mom got a job at the serpentarium exhibit where she'd give tours of snakes and other reptiles, and my older brother, Chuck, worked at the jungle exhibit. As for me, I was assigned to the rare-birds farm. They would import birds and we would quarantine them until they were ready to sell off to other zoos. My younger sister and brother were too young to work. It was summertime, and I'm not sure who watched them while we were all on the job, but knowing Mother, she had something creative worked out.

Summer came and went, and it was time for Chuck and me to start junior high school. Chuck wanted to be in the same grade as me, so he backed up a year so that we'd be in the same class. We were always close—never jealous or envious of one another. There's absolutely nothing like the bond of family, and ours had been strengthened further by the loss of our father and the move.

Every day after school, I would take care of parrots, flamingos, and storks. Not only was it a fantastic job opportunity, but it was also a lot of fun. I loved working closely with the exotic birds. I worked as much as possible, staying at the zoo off and on for several years.

When I was in high school, the manager asked for a volunteer to help transport a waddle of penguins from the zoo in Miami to the Columbus Zoo. I would be returning to my hometown for a business trip. I jumped at the chance. The next thing I knew, I was in a train boxcar, traveling more than 1,200 miles with about six penguins. To keep them comfortable, I would ice down their wings and make sure the car didn't overheat. It was an exciting assignment, and the trip sparked that same intoxicating feeling of freedom and adventure that I had felt on the train to the Indianapolis Speedway.

When I arrived back in Columbus, everyone was buzzing about the arrival of "Penrod's penguins." I didn't hate the attention. While I was still at the Columbus Zoo, the newest national celebrity arrived: Colo, the first gorilla to be born in captivity. Named after the city of Columbus, Colo quickly became an international sensation. She was the perfect story for the new medium of television news.

The cameramen fought to get footage of the four-pound celebrity. She even ended up on the cover of *Life* magazine. Colo's mother had rejected her, so she had to be hand-raised by the zookeepers like a human child. She was dressed in clothing and fed from a bottle. Because I worked with animals, I was allowed to hold her—at the very moment when a photographer from the *Columbus Dispatch* was there to take pictures. Colo and I ended up on the front page of the newspaper. I always seemed to be in the right place at the right time.

I soon returned to Florida to continue my work and reunite with my family. Things were changing once again. Mother hated being alone. She came from an era when women were expected to be married. Besides, she was still in her early thirties, and she was beautiful. Not long after we arrived in Florida, she started dating—and had no shortage of suitors.

Before entering high school, I really wanted to attend this nearby school that won all the state football championships. The coach wanted me to come play too. But my mom ended up marrying a guy who worked with Florida Power and Light, and they moved to be closer to the Keys where he was a line man. So we were the first class to ever go to school at South Dade County High School. We played the school I wanted to go to in the Orange Bowl that first year and we lost 48 - 0. But I didn't let the loss get to me. I knew high school was a passing phase.

My mother had three more children with her new husband—my half-siblings. But things soured between them quickly. My stepfather was an alcoholic, and he was an angry drunk. Whenever he drank, he was verbally abusive to Mother. It was the first time I saw the effects of alcohol abuse up close. I quickly grew to hate the chaos of drunkenness. I vowed to never let alcohol get the best of me.

School was never really my thing, but I enrolled at South Dade High School in Homestead. In addition to my part-time jobs, I decided to focus on athletics. One of my teachers was the track coach, and he correctly surmised I would be a fast runner. After a little bit of convincing, I tried out for the team. I was somewhat surprised to make the roster—a kid never really knows if he's fast or not. But as it turned out, I was.

The track coach also worked with the football team, and he explained the possibilities of the sport. I had no intention of going to college—I already knew how to make money. But the idea of being offered a scholarship didn't sound terrible. Plus, I had noticed how much the girls liked football players. I enjoyed the camaraderie of the team. I'd never had many friends my own age. Sports were both an outlet and a teacher to me. They taught me discipline, gave me a purpose, and maybe most importantly, they kept me out of trouble and helped me graduate high school.

At South Dade High, the teachers were more lenient with athletes than they were with the rest of the student body. No one ever made any academic demand of me. I graduated with average grades. During those years, the school was primarily known for educating farmers—it offered agricultural classes in addition to the core academic requirements. Because I had no desire to ever be a farmer, I didn't see the importance of immersing myself in my studies. But I did enjoy learning how to drive a tractor.

Since my high school days, I have grown to understand the importance of education. I can appreciate and admire the work ethic it takes to finish and succeed in college. I don't think higher education is a requirement for significant achievement, but it can provide you with a springboard to success. I told my kids that if they didn't go to college, they had to learn a trade. They're all mostly grown now, and I still stand by that philosophy.

But at the time, school simply wasn't my top priority. I would hang out with my football buddies and the cheerleaders. Their favorite pastime was to go out and get drunk. But I stood firm in my decision not to drink. Despite all the peer pressure, I didn't have a sip of alcohol until I was 21 years old. From my view, alcohol was a distraction from what mattered most—winning trophies and making money. So while I would often go out with them, I never bothered with getting drunk. I still had a lot of fun in high school, but I preferred to enjoy it sober.

After living in Florida for about two years, my family's living arrangements improved once again. My mother's father died the year after we left Ohio; in 1955, her mother passed away, and their estate was liquidated. The Columbus duplex I had once called home was put on the market. My mother got about $35,000 when it sold—a life-changing amount of money in the 1950s. With the windfall, she bought five acres of land in Perrine—an entire block. There was a main house and three small buildings on the property. Chuck and I claimed one of those sheds for our own. We patched the ceiling and paneled the walls. It became our very own "bachelor pad."

When my mother worked at the snake sanctuary, I found out that if you caught a snake and brought it in, they'd pay you a dollar a foot for it. So I'd wade out into the swamps of South Florida with a burlap bag—with water up to my neck—and I'd catch snakes to sell. Some of these snakes I ended up keeping. I remember one yellow python in particular that I decided to make my pet. He was beautiful, and he lived in the rafters of our shed for a while before scurrying back off to the wild.

By this time, my mother had divorced her second husband and was married again. They started a business installing TVs and TV antennas. I worked for them whenever I could, and I eventually saved up enough money to buy my first car. The ticket price was a hefty $75. I loved that car. But more than the car itself, I loved the independence it offered me. No more walking and no more hitching rides. I could further rely on myself, which I knew was always the best bet.

I know what you're thinking: *You were old enough to drive a car?*

Yes and no. Legally, no way. I was 14 years old, and my mom had to lie about my age so that I could get a license. Back then, all you needed was for a parent to sign a piece of paper, so it really wasn't a big deal. I was also working at the Golden Rule Grocery Store delivering groceries. I worked mostly for tips, so timeliness was essential. The license and car were both necessities. Plus, I was a great driver. I was cautious and conscientious.

What I wasn't, however, was a trained diver. But I've always been able to hold my breath like one. I used to be able to hold my breath for 3 minutes and 20 seconds. Now it's probably no longer than two, but I used to be able to dive and swim without any equipment for a significant amount of time.

At the same time that I was delivering groceries in Homestead, I also started selling fresh fish out of the trunk of my car. I had an inner tube that I put a wire net in, and I attached it to a long rope. I would swim out to this reef, and I'd stay in the water up to 14 hours, snagging fish and putting them in a basket I brought along—because the sharks would swarm if you didn't take the fish out of the water.

I'd put the fish on ice in the trunk of my car, and I'd go into different cities and sell fresh fish at a lower cost than the markets. I made a decent amount of money as an inner-tube fisherman!

Most teenagers would have abused the freedom I had with my own place and my own car, but I had known for some time that my life had a greater purpose. I don't know if I *knew* that or *decided* that—it was just a reality to me. I continued to work hard at a series of high school jobs.

When I was 15, I worked as a waiter at the Dog N' Suds, a drive-in style restaurant that served hot dogs and root beer. I wore roller skates to bring trays out to the cars. It was my first job in food service. But it wouldn't be my last.

The most rewarding high school job I had was as a lifeguard at the local community pool during the summer. When I was 16, I saw a young boy lying motionless on the bottom of the pool. I dragged him out of the water. As a crowd gathered, I gave him CPR until he began breathing again. As the adrenaline continued to flow through my body, I felt like a hero—until the boy's mother approached me. Her face was twisted into a scowl.

"How could you let this happen?" she snapped at me.

I stared at her for a minute, dumbfounded at her anger. "But I just saved his life," I pointed out.

The mother didn't reply but turned around and flounced off with her son in tow. I stared at her as she left, unsure of why she lashed out at me. Despite her anger, I was proud of my actions, and I felt like I had been put at the pool that day for a reason. Even as a teenager, I realized she wasn't really angry at me but was upset at the fact she had almost lost her son. It was easier to yell at me than to face the reality of what had almost happened. I expected she would someday come back and thank me for heroically saving her son, but she never did. I never saw her—or the boy—again.

Although the mother was incredibly rude, she taught me a valuable lesson that day. For the rest of my life, I would understand the importance of doing the right thing whether I thought other people would appreciate it or not. People may misunderstand my actions or motives, but in the end, it doesn't matter what other people think. What matters is that I can live with myself for the decisions I make. In reality, the mother probably grew to be grateful I saved her son's life. She just never bothered to thank me.

Around this time, I started working at a filling station. Cars would pull up and I would fill their tanks with gasoline and clean their windows and windshields. I don't know if you've ever spent time in South Florida, but a notable characteristic of the climate is the overwhelming presence of bugs. It was impossible to clean off all the bugs with the bucket of soap and sponge they gave me. I decided to get creative. I got some pieces of corn on the cob and used them in place of the sponge. The bugs came right off. Before long, the line of cars to get the "cob" treatment stretched through the parking lot.

I guess the idea spread through word-of-mouth, because soon it seemed as if every filling station in the area started using cobs of corn to clean bugs off windshields and headlights. It wasn't long until someone developed a sponge to mimic a cob of corn. They were being used everywhere—on cars and boats alike.

My home life was finally stable. And as I headed into my senior year, I continued to work hard. I took any odd job that would earn me a few extra dollars. I never had trouble balancing my sports schedule, social life, and work. I had more than enough energy for them all. That hasn't really changed to this day. When it's all you ever know, anything less feels strange.

Chuck and I graduated in 1957. I got an invitation to try out for the University of Miami football team. I went there for summer training, but I couldn't figure out how I was going to get rich playing football. In those days, professional players just made a living—they didn't earn the fortunes they get paid today. I was 180 pounds and very fast, but they brought in all these enormous players from Pittsburgh. One of my *least* favorite exercises was something they called "chicken circle." They'd put all the giants in a circle with me standing alone in the middle. It was my job to find my way out.

Needless to say, I decided to make my millions another way. Not that I didn't walk away from football without a couple of souvenirs—I have two metal knees now that invite a flurry of TSA activity every time I fly. I would have preferred a championship ring, but that just wasn't in the cards for me.

Chuck and I had originally planned to join the military together. After he enlisted, I had a change of heart. I decided to go off into the world and start making some money. He always gave me a good-natured hard time for not serving at the same time as him, but it ultimately turned out to be the right decision.

I was now 18, and I knew it was time for me to leave Homestead in search of my next adventure. I sold my car and hitchhiked the two-hour trip down to the Florida Keys.

A new chapter of my life was about to begin. It was time to make that first million.

SMILIN' JACK

"When I was younger, I got the nickname 'Smilin' Jack' because I always had a pleasant look on my face. My optimistic outlook showed. My attitude helped me advance in my jobs and meet new people. A smile and a happy disposition are great assets to have—not only when you're young, but throughout your life."

—JACK

Despite our poverty and the loss of my father, I had a wonderful childhood. When I look back, what stands out are memories of sports, my siblings, and a mother who loved us all unconditionally. We never went hungry, we always had a roof over our heads, and there was always an opportunity to work and improve our situation.

But I wasn't a kid anymore. I was 18, and it was time to see what else the world had to offer Jack Penrod.

As I headed down the bridges into the Florida Keys, I grew increasingly excited about my future. Uncertainty had never really bothered me before. To me, the unknown was just another opportunity to create an adventure. I had confidence everything would work out, and I was energized about truly being on my own. Although I had grown up with fewer parental rules than most kids, this was the first time I would have no adult oversight. My success was completely up to me. I wasn't the least bit worried—it never occurred to me I could possibly fail.

When I arrived in the Keys, I knocked on every door, looking for a job. When I knocked on the door of the Cabana Club on Key Colony Beach in Marathon, Florida, I knew I had stumbled on my next opportunity. I quickly talked my way into a job. I would earn a small salary, get a furnished room to sleep in, and keep all the tips I could get from the rich guests. I would clean the pool, set out mats and towels, and interact with the guests to make sure they were having a good time. It was a perfect job for me. I could earn some money and enjoy a considerable amount of free time.

But I learned rather quickly I wouldn't be content with a whole lot of "free" time. Time spent not making money felt like time wasted. I needed something more to do, and I knew there was plenty of work for industrious kids like me. I found out that the restaurant next door needed a dishwasher. I said, "I'll do it." I was only working days at the Cabana Club, so I started washing dishes at the Shamrock, a seafood restaurant, at night.

I washed dishes like a madman. I never took breaks, and those pots and pans never looked so clean. I guess the higher-ups noticed, because it wasn't long before they were asking me if I wanted a job in the dining room as a host. I'd refill water glasses and help clear empty plates from tables. Before the summer was over, I'd been promoted to *maître d'*—me, an 18-year-old kid from Columbus, Ohio, serving Caesar salads and cutting Chateaubriand at the tables.

It was during these jobs at the Cabana Club and the Shamrock that I began to understand the hospitality industry. People would fork over their money to enjoy good service. Give them *great* service? You could line your pockets with tips. I also recognized that I had a knack for anticipating the needs and wants of guests. I learned that if you could give someone something they didn't know they needed, you had a loyal fan for life.

I met a lot of great people working at the Cabana Club. I missed my family, but I knew I was doing the best thing for all of us. I had made that promise to my mother, after all, and I intended to make good on it. Besides, this work was my *ipso facto* college education.

It actually was a celebrity who gave me my next opportunity. I was working poolside at the Cabana Club when I met a petite divorcee in her early forties who seemed to enjoy my company. Her name was Katherine Rawls. I soon learned she was an Olympic swimmer and diver who had won nearly forty championships in various national competitions and had even medaled three times in the Olympics.

Katherine's success had made her a household name in the thirties and forties. She was more than just a celebrity. Americans thought of her as a national treasure. She was short—just five foot, two inches—and the newspapers had dubbed her "The Minnow." She was a media darling and knew how to tell fascinating stories about her glamorous career.

When she was just 14, Katherine had become an international sensation at the U.S. National Championships when she upset two world champions in swimming races. The following year, during the

1932 Summer Olympics in Los Angeles, she took home the silver medal. In 1937, she was named Female Athlete of the Year.

As if that weren't impressive enough, Katherine was also one of the initial 28 pilots who formed the Women's Auxiliary Ferrying Squadron in 1942, stationed in Detroit, transporting military cargo by air as part of the U.S. war effort. She had traveled around the world several times and had stories about her adventures in Germany, Japan, and Australia.

I was impressed by all her accomplishments.

Katherine liked me. Although she was based in Florida, working at the Cabana Club in the fall and winter, she traveled to West Virginia each summer to manage the aquatics division at the Greenbrier, a luxury resort and hotel outside White Sulphur Springs. Katherine gave swim lessons and planned swimming and diving exhibitions all summer long, and she needed a staff to work the poolside with her. My job would include serving food and setting up lounge chairs— very similar work to what I was doing at the Cabana Club, but for more money. The clientele would be even more upscale, and I would probably get better tips. Plus, I'd never been to West Virginia. I jumped at the chance for my next adventure.

But first I had a promise to keep. With virtually no personal bills to pay, I had made enough money working two jobs to pay cash for a Chevrolet convertible—and to pay off my mother's house. At that time, she was working in a restaurant serving breakfast and making coffee. It was an $18,000 payoff, and it was the last of what I had saved. But I didn't mind. I was a man of my word. Plus, I knew there was far more money to be made.

The first time I saw the Greenbrier, I finally understood what luxury really was. A stately white building set against lush, green grass, the resort was impressive in both its size and its finery. Built around a spring of sulphur water in 1778 , the property had gone through a massive expansion and upgrade in the early twentieth century, becoming the preeminent destination for the rich and famous.

Its annual summer opening was the social event of the season, attracting government leaders, business tycoons, and celebrities. Twenty-six presidents had stayed at the resort, and it was a common destination for the entire Kennedy family. In 1958, it was the top resort hotel in the world. I would be meeting a new caliber of people, and it would be important for me to stand out.

I was originally hired for poolside duties and was doing very well. I earned $50 a day in tips—more than $400 in today's money. Like the Cabana Club, the Greenbrier offered me a nice place to live and free meals. The income was good, and the surroundings were breathtaking. For many people, this would have been the pinnacle of what they could achieve. For me, however, I had my sights set on more.

Working the pool for tips would not give me the training I needed. Although I hadn't gone to college, I realized that, in a way, I was in my own university. I had the chance to learn new things. I didn't want to squander it.

After work, the young people my age would go into the woods to drink and party. Because that didn't interest me, I went to the personnel department and asked for additional responsibilities to do during my spare time. I wanted to learn everything about running a successful resort.

Eventually, I found work in the kitchen. My first job there was to take a blow torch to sear the steaks and lock in their juice and flavor. Then I'd pass it down the line to be cooked. I also made salads—I was the steak and salad guy. Before long, the hotel president noticed me. He asked if I wanted to work some hours at the front desk. Of course I agreed.

On my first day, the guy training me said, "The trick of this job is learning to say, 'Kiss my ass,' with a smile on your face." But for the most part, the guests at the Greenbrier were great people.

My diverse responsibilities gave me an overview of hotel operations. I had no idea then how important this knowledge would someday be.

While working the long, hot hours in the kitchen, I met Chef Rouche, one of the world-famous Golden Dozen chefs. I had never seen such a master in the kitchen. He was an artist, making giant sculptures, like castles, out of butter. Coming from my background, it was amazing that people had the resources to create works of art out of food. I was captivated.

The general manager of the Greenbrier was a young and dynamic man named Truman Wright. Truman was just 36 years old when I started working at the resort. He was good, competent, polished, and a natural-born leader. With a hands-on approach and a decisive personality, Truman was everything I wanted to be in life.

One day near the end of summer, he pulled me into his office. "When I was young," he began, "I didn't have the money for college. An older man paid to send me to Cornell, but I had to promise him I would do the same for another young man when I could afford it. So I'd like to offer to pay for you to go to Cornell."

I stared at him in a moment of stunned silence before I replied, "What's Cornell?"

"It's one of the best colleges in the country," Truman replied, with a smile. "With a Cornell degree, you could do anything you want to do. You could even become the general manager of the Greenbrier."

"I don't know," I replied skeptically. "I have never thought much about college before. How much money could I earn as the general manager here?"

Truman's eyes met mine. "You could make $25,000 per year," he said proudly. "But there are so many other benefits. I don't pay a mortgage. I don't have to pay for meals. It's a wonderful living."

I thought for a minute. I knew $25,000 was a staggering amount of money in 1957—roughly equivalent to $208,000 in today's dollars—but I remembered my promise to Mother. I had promised her I would become a millionaire, and I didn't see any possible way to get that rich on a $25,000 salary. I made a decision that was either very gutsy or very stupid.

"I appreciate the offer," I earnestly told Truman, "but I have different goals, and I don't think I can get there as the general manager of the Greenbrier. I'm going to have to turn down your offer."

To his credit, Truman respected my decision and never questioned me, and I never regretted it. The Greenbrier was a place where people stayed for a very long time. Another kid named Jack began working in the resort the same year I did and was there for *50 years*. I wouldn't be content standing still, and I didn't want to become complacent.

I received other offers during my time at the Greenbrier from other people who had noticed my ambition and hard work. A dentist who was ready to retire told me he would give me his entire practice if I went to college to study dentistry. There were two things wrong with his proposal. First—and most importantly—I had no interest in the medical field. I couldn't imagine standing with my hands in someone's mouth all day.

Second, I didn't like the financial ramifications of dentistry. I knew that a medical practice would only earn money during the hours I was working. If I wasn't there, no money would be made. I was looking for a line of work with passive income. I wanted to build a successful business that would outlast my life, that I could pass down to my family. I may have only been 18, but I knew my own mind. I was just stubborn enough. A dentistry practice just wasn't going to work out.

During that first summer at the Greenbrier, I didn't have to be at work until late morning. With little else to do, I would walk around the property to see what was going on. I soon gravitated toward the golf course where legendary golfer Sam Snead was the pro. I would watch some of the PGA legends as they practiced on the lush links of the Greenbrier course. Golfers like Gary Player, Ben Hogan, and Jack Nicklaus would regularly hold tournaments on one of the Greenbrier's four golf courses. I was most drawn to Jack Nicklaus. He was just seven months younger than I was. It was inspiring to watch the young golf legend at the beginning of his career.

When you're surrounded by greatness, it's easy to miss the life lessons they can teach. Watching the professional golfers play, I saw examples of patience and tenacity. One day I watched Sam shoot a 59 in tournament play. After such a good game, an inferior player would have retired to the clubhouse for a drink, but Sam went back to the practice tee and hit the same shot again and again. Suddenly his remarkable consistency wasn't as mysterious. He had trained himself into consistent excellence. A true professional may make things look effortless, but it's usually an illusion. Success takes a lot of behind-the-scenes practice and determination.

While I was impressed by Sam Snead's discipline, I was less than a fan of his personality. He was often grumpy and abrupt and had a reputation for being impatient and unkind. Women were attracted to his success. He would play against amateurs and handicap himself by using nothing but a putter. He would beat them soundly and would be arrogant about his win.

At the Greenbrier, employees were allowed to play on one of the golf courses, so I would play 18 or 36 holes each day. I used a steel shaft and was soon able to hit the ball more than 300 yards. Studying the golfers play, I was inspired to hone my game to a six handicap. I saw golf as a worthy pursuit to invest in. More deals are closed on golf courses than in boardrooms. I knew it was a skill that would one day allow me to invest in strategic relationships to network.

I loved everything about working at the Greenbrier. Sometime during my first summer there, I caught the eye of a 42-year-old woman named Barbara "Bobo" Sears Rockefeller—a coal miner's daughter who had married well and divorced even better. Born to Lithuanian immigrants in Pittsburgh, Bobo had grown up in a poor Chicago tenement near the stockyards. A former Miss Lithuania, in her younger days Bobo had been a successful stage actress and top model who appeared in the pages of *Vogue* and *Vanity Fair*.

Bobo had lived an interesting life. Her first marriage was to a man named Richard Sears, Jr., the son of a prominent Boston family. While married to Richard, Bobo was named third secretary at the American embassy in Paris, where she and Richard became fixtures in the Parisian social scene. Six years later, the two divorced. Then, on midnight of Valentine's Day in 1948, Bobo married Winthrop Rockefeller—Manhattan's most eligible bachelor and an heir to the Standard Oil fortune—in Palm Beach. The ceremony was billed as the "Cinderella Wedding of the Century." Their only child, Winthrop, Jr., was born just seven months later—a fact that kept tongues wagging in society circles.

Winthrop, Sr., was the governor of Arkansas, and Bobo was the embodiment of a well-heeled socialite and politician's wife. There were no traces of her hardscrabble upbringing—she was completely at home with the old money of the Rockefellers. She had trained herself to fit in.

But the marriage wasn't a happy one, and it collapsed within two years of the wedding. In 1951, Bobo filed for divorce. The media would show up at her door unannounced, and she would happily give interviews about her husband, accusing him of humiliating her before the world. Winthrop settled with her in 1954 for $5.5 million, a record-breaking figure at the time. In today's economy, her settlement would be worth more than $52 million.

Bobo knew how to handle herself in any situation. She taught herself divorce law by reading legal journals and case law. Her lawyers, annoyed at her hands-on approach, frequently quit. She went through more than 20 attorneys in the first year of her divorce. As a woman publicly scorned, she quickly figured out the deadliest weapon in her arsenal was the media.

During a 1952 interview with *Time* magazine, she was bitterly candid. "I intend to be Mrs. Rockefeller until the day I die," she said. True to her word, she never reverted to her maiden name. Winthrop married again in 1956; the marriage would also end in divorce.

In 1958, Bobo arrived at the Greenbrier with a young Winthrop, Jr. He was a thoughtful and well-mannered nine-year-old boy. Both Bobo and Winthrop took an instant liking to me, so I was always available to them. As her stay came to an end, Bobo approached me. "Have you ever been to New York?" she asked.

"No, I haven't."

"Would you like to come for a visit?"

Since the Greenbrier was only open in the summer, I had nowhere else in particular to go. New York sounded like *the* place for adventure. "That sounds fun," I told her.

At the end of the summer, I headed to Manhattan. As an adult, I would probably hesitate to show up at a socialite's home unannounced, but something was different about my relationship with Bobo. I felt comfortable with her. I knocked on the heavy door at her home. A maid answered and ushered me into the grandest home I had ever seen in my life.

With her divorce settlement, Bobo had bought a seven-story brownstone—which sounds more modest than what it was. Bobo's home was a lavish, 10,000-square-foot mansion at 13 E. 67th Street in Manhattan, right beside Central Park. It was gaudily tricked out with tapestries, murals, and mirrors. In an alcove, there was even a life-sized statue of Pan, the Greek god of nature. With the 19-foot ceilings, a squash court, and a pool, the mansion embodied what I thought wealth was. I walked into the foyer and thought I felt tall grass tickling my ankles. As it turned out, I was standing on plush carpet. There was seemingly no end to the home's customizations. It had become one of Manhattan's most sought-after destinations.

Bobo was very happy to see me. She showed me to my room and then invited me to come downstairs for dinner. Sitting at the large table, I was given a goblet to drink from. As I sipped from it, I guess I was squeezing it. It felt both heavy and soft.

"Careful," Bobo warned. "That's pure gold. We wouldn't want to bend it."

Bobo was showing off for me a little, I guess, but a country boy like me from Homestead didn't have any concept of what pure gold was. I was certain I'd never encountered it before. I stared at the goblet in wonder.

Starry-eyed at the ostentatious display of wealth, I sent a letter to my mother, who was still living in our modest Homestead house. "Dear Mother," I began. "It's not so bad to be rich." I stayed there for a few days. As I got ready to leave, Bobo offered me a job.

"I want you to be Winnie's guardian," she said.

I had already found out that nine-year-old Winthrop had a bank account and was studying languages I had never heard of. It was beyond my capacity to tutor him, but Bobo's requirement was clear: spend time with Winthrop and teach him how to be a man. I could check that box, so I accepted the job immediately, knowing I could always return to the Greenbrier the following summer.

Bobo ran an antique company of sorts from the house. She was a collector herself, and there was a constant stream of staff connected to her antique dealings going in and out of the house. I noticed that all the staff were gay men. It dawned on me that Bobo kept the company of gay men for two reasons: (1) she preferred them, and (2) she felt safe with them. There was never a chance of her falling in love and getting hurt again.

My arrival at the Rockefeller home was a much-discussed topic among the socialites. Many people believed that I was Bobo's "boy." She certainly wouldn't be the first wealthy divorcee who got herself a young male escort. Even my brothers believed—and still believe—

there was a physical relationship between Bobo and me. But they are wrong. I was an 18-year-old kid and she was a lady in her forties. I know Bobo enjoyed my company—and I enjoyed hers—but my life with the Rockefellers was strictly platonic and professional.

Trust me, Bobo wasn't lonely. She had plenty of dates with handsome young men who were only too happy to take her out and be seen on her arm. I remember one night she came home from one of those dates and I had been sitting in the library, reading. Bobo's library was massive. It had every important title and probably every almost-important title too. I learned to love reading there.

Which is why, when she walked in the house, I hadn't heard her arrive. I was sitting in my underwear, engrossed in a book. *That* was a pickle I had to wiggle my way out of. She must have told her employees, because they all approached me. "You could have been rich, you know. You could have been her lover."

I could have, but I didn't. Not because she wasn't beautiful, but because I had principles. I had values and morals. We weren't particularly religious growing up, but I did belong to the Church of God and had been baptized in the Ohio River. I pray before I eat, but I'd rather live a life that demonstrates my faith more than I tell people what to do. I want to lead by example.

All that being said, I did meet a girl while I was in New York, from RKO Dress Design. I actually met a few girls. It seemed like models were everywhere in Manhattan. And they all wanted to visit the third floor of Barbara Rockefeller's home—the floor she had given me full reign of.

There was only one problem with the situation, at least as far as Bobo was concerned. I didn't look the part of the Rockefeller world. I had arrived wearing a blazer with a sweater underneath it. "That won't do," Bobo said. "Especially if we want to get you into the black book. Let's get you looking like a New Yorker."

I had no idea what the black book was, but I knew Bobo was right—especially with fall and winter approaching New York. She immediately sent me to Brooks Brothers to get the "right" clothes. Her tailor made sure everything fit me in a way that would be acceptable to Bobo. She taught me the importance of looking the part. When you're dressed nicely, people assume you're successful and are more likely to give you an opportunity. Plus, people just treat you better.

Bobo would throw larger-than-life parties for the New York social scene. I used to come downstairs and people watch. There were people putting cigarettes out on the rug and spilling wine on the antique furniture. The parties were both lavish and crazy. The next morning, the house would be trashed. Bobo didn't care. She had more than enough money to fix whatever had been broken. She had more money than she knew what to do with.

Officially, my job was to look after Winthrop, Jr., whom I called Winnie. I was his friend, his guardian, his menu planner, and his social scheduler. I would set up play dates, plan his meals, and ensure he had an appointment to eat dinner with Bobo at least once a week.

Winnie was groomed from an early age to take over the family fortune. He was educated in both the U.S. and abroad. His father was the sole heir to the entire fortune and Junior was his only son, and the favorite grandson of John D. He was exposed to business, banking, and multiple languages from a very early age. Nothing about Winnie was left to chance—he was going to take over the fortune and manage it well.

Bobo and Winnie had this oversized standard poodle. Once I decided what Winnie and I were going to eat, I'd write down what meat we'd need on a note and I'd attach it to her neck. Then this dog would walk next door to the butcher. The butcher would read the note, cut the meat, and send it back around the poodle's neck. I'd never seen anything like it then, and I haven't seen anything like it since. That dog was a legend!

I took Winnie to school and helped him with his homework. I was surprised how hands-off Bobo was in parenting her son. She had more than enough time to spend with him, but she would rather have others look after him. It was a sharp contrast from my own mother, who longed to spend more time with her children.

If the weather was nice, I'd take Winnie out to Central Park, and we'd let the dog run around and chase insects. Speaking of chases, there were a few times Winnie and I were chased by down-on-their-luck people who called Central Park their home. I don't know if they recognized him as a Rockefeller or if we just had bad luck. I was never scared for myself, but I found myself fiercely protective of Winnie. He was just a kid in a grown-up's world, trying his best to be normal. I felt for him. I learned to watch our backs everywhere we went.

By springtime, Bobo was begging me to go with Winnie to Arkansas for the summer—that's when Winnie spent time with his father. But I had no interest in being around that guy, so I politely declined. Later I would find out that Winnie broke his arm that summer and cried for me. "Jack, Jack," he wailed. "I only want Jack!"

But I wasn't there. I had made the drive back to West Virginia for another three months of the Greenbrier. Truthfully, I felt Winnie and I had grown too close. He was attached to me—the first adult to ever give him attention. I didn't think it was healthy; I knew I would never be a permanent fixture in his life.

When winter came again, Bobo asked me to return. I told her I couldn't do it. So she sent me a brand-new car, a bright red convertible Austin-Healey, and said, "Will you please come back?" So I went back in a new car. But that was my last winter in Manhattan. I was 20 years old then, and it was time for me to move on.

I'd heard about this hamburger place selling a burger, fries, and a coke for 42 cents. I thought, *This is the future.* I had no idea how right I was.

A MCDONALD'S EDUCATION

"Everything important I learned about business, I learned inside a McDonald's."
—JACK

I spent two summers at the Greenbrier and two winters with the Rockefellers. I'd wallowed in the wealth of my surroundings and rubbed shoulders with celebrities, politicians, models, and millionaires. By the time I was 20, I needed a change of scenery. The country boy from Homestead needed to cleanse his palette.

I could also sense the pressures of entering my twenties from all sides. It wasn't a terrible feeling—I've always liked pressure. But I knew it wouldn't be long until I chose a career path and pursued it. I wanted one more season of being a kid. So my buddy Cliff and I decided to open our own chicken farm.

There was this Cuban gentleman who already had a farm with 10,000 chickens. It was right inside of Homestead, and it had three screen homes and one groundhouse. The man asked Cliff and me if we'd take over the farm for him. I'm sure it comes as no surprise that my first thought was, *Here we go . . . a new adventure!*

So, without any training or knowledge as to what we were doing, we set about figuring out what we'd gotten ourselves into. We learned how to clean the cages, gather the eggs, and pack the eggs. Our sign out front had a suggestive slogan: All of Our Chicks Lay. And, you know, it was making money. We were doing okay.

It was a completely different world than my time at the Rockefeller mansion, but it was a good experience—working without a boss. Cliff and I made all the decisions. I hired my younger brother, Bob, at $25 a week to do the work I didn't want to do. We had the hubris of youth—we threw a lot of parties and met a lot of girls. We also sought out new moneymaking opportunities. I had heard how farming could be lucrative and decided to start planting tomatoes and corn on the property, using the chicken manure as fertilizer. (Bob thinks we made him scoop the manure out from all the chicken cages. He was probably right.) It was an opportunity to make a good living, and I felt we were riding high.

But one thing we couldn't control was the weather. On September 10, 1960, South Florida was hit by Hurricane Donna, a category-five storm with 160-mile-per-hour winds. The storm devastated South Florida's economy—destroying 50 percent of the citrus crop and flooding the coastlines. The chicken ranch was covered in four feet of water. We had to keep the chickens in their cages and keep the manure from piling up. We were doing everything we could to keep our heads above water—figuratively and literally.

Finally, Cliff and I agreed that it was time to move on. The chickens weren't laying eggs, and we were still paying to feed them. The crops were gone. The former owner wasn't giving us any money to cover costs, and we were no longer profitable. We had no choice but to close up shop and move on. It was just as well. My life's goal wasn't to be a farmer. They tend to live poor and die rich, when my life goal was very different. We called the Cuban man and said, "It's all yours," and walked away.

I had enjoyed my chicken ranching days, but I wasn't too disappointed when they came to an end. As I said, I had found this restaurant in South Florida that sold an entire meal for less than 50 cents. It looked like the next big thing, and I wanted to work there. The name of the restaurant was McDonald's.

I first heard of McDonald's when they opened at Florida State College on West Tennessee Street. For all my talk about not seeing the value of college, that's exactly where I ended up after the chicken farm. Cliff's mom had called us and said, "Why don't you boys move in with me here in Tallahassee? You can stay rent free and go to college."

I became a Seminole. When that McDonald's opened, Cliff and I both went in to apply. They hired us both

During the 1950s, Americans, especially teenagers, flocked to diners for inexpensive hamburgers, fries, and shakes. Restaurants popped up across the American landscape, many of them with similar menus. It was a winning formula. There was nothing particularly novel about McDonald's except for their quality. The food was good. The restaurants were clean. The people were friendly.

McDonald's had first started in the early 1940s in California. The brainchild of the McDonald brothers, the restaurant's menu included barbecued pork, chicken, and ribs. Eventually, the brothers realized most of their money came from their hamburger sales. They revised their business plan and dropped all the barbecue items from the menu. Their volume skyrocketed. Soon the brothers began running their kitchen like an assembly line to meet their growing demand. To make their famous desserts, they used a multi-mixer milkshake machine they had bought from a businessman named Ray Kroc.

Ray was a visionary. He was always open to new ideas, yet he demanded perfection in everything he did. In 1954, when he was 51, he checked out McDonald's for the first time—and liked what he found. When he tasted the burgers, Ray knew he had found the next big thing. He met with the McDonald brothers and convinced them to let him franchise the restaurant. He opened his first restaurant in Des Plaines, Illinois. As the restaurant became popular, Ray was ready to take it to the next level. The McDonald brothers, however, were satisfied with their current volume. By 1961, Ray had bought the entire company for $2.7 million.

I had my first McDonald's hamburger in 1960 and thought the quality was excellent. Like Ray Kroc, I was also very impressed with the business model of the restaurant. They could hire employees with little or no culinary experience and turn them into cooks. It was a beautifully simple concept.

I was only 21 years old, but I had chosen my path—I was going to make a career out of McDonald's. Cliff and I hadn't yet started school, so all of our focus was on making money. The pay was 85 cents an hour—much less than I had earned at my previous jobs.

Despite the low wage, I instinctively knew McDonald's was going to be something really big. I thought, eventually, I would be able to make a lot of money. Together, Cliff and I both began our hard work at McDonald's. Our goal was to get promoted.

We didn't have to wait long. Cliff and I were a different caliber than many of the other employees. While they looked at the restaurant as just another job, we looked at it as a career. We took a lot of pride in our work and went above and beyond what we were asked to do.

The owner of the Tallahassee McDonald's was Jerry Olson, a retired Chrysler dealer out of Chicago. He had been an old friend of the McDonald's owner Ray Kroc and had invested a considerable amount of money into opening some of the first franchises. He was a hands-off owner. He didn't want to spend every day in the restaurant. Instead, he largely relied on other people to make his money for him.

Jerry liked Cliff and me; we had the hustle he valued in his workers. The store was being managed by a guy who had been to school and gotten formal training for the job. But they caught him stealing on the very first day and fired him. Jerry came up to Cliff and me and said, "You boys think you can run this place?"

We looked at each other, knowing neither of us had any experience in management or fast-food service. "Sure," we said. "We can run it."

Within three days of our employment, Jerry had promoted us both to co-managers. We were each given a salary of $125 per week. In today's dollars, that would be a $51,000-a-year job—and I was still in my early twenties. The store quickly became enormously busy. Cliff and I continued to work long hours, learning every aspect of the business.

Maybe Tallahassee was an odd choice for me to make my fortune. Had I known more about the city, I might never have moved there. Despite it being Florida's capital, Tallahassee was a sleepy town of 40,000 people—mostly farmers and blue-collar workers. The year I arrived in town, there had been a movement to move the capital to Orlando, closer to the population center. Tallahassee was not an up-and-coming city; it was old Florida. There was nothing upscale about it.

But even in smaller cities, there are opportunities to be found. In addition to the state government, there was a demographic that was largely underserved at the restaurants around town. Florida State University was one of the country's fastest growing universities, populated by thousands of students who were short on money yet willing to eat at restaurants. These students would be the target demographic of my McDonald's. If I were going to succeed anywhere on the Florida panhandle, a college town made the most sense.

As I immersed myself into my work, I knew there were certain outside forces that might derail my success. America was in the midst of the Vietnam War, one of the darkest periods of the twentieth century. As the conflict escalated, there was a threat that the U.S. would institute a military draft and I could be chosen to fight overseas. If I volunteered before I was drafted, my time in the service would be much shorter. Cliff, on the other hand, had reasons of his own that made it so he *couldn't* be drafted.

I went to Jerry with a proposal. "I can wait until I'm drafted," I said to him, "or I can go in for six months now. But if I wait until I'm drafted, I might end up overseas for a lot longer than six months."

He thought it over. "I recommend going in for six months and getting it out of the way," he said. "There will still be a job waiting for you when you come back."

Although I was worried about my career, I was happy to serve my country. I enlisted in the Marine Corps in 1962 and was sent to Paris Island, South Carolina, for boot camp. I had heard stories that painted the experience as rough and tumble. But to me, it was all a game. I loved it.

You've seen the military movies, right? Where some baldheaded guy is always yelling at the recruits? I got off the bus and that's exactly what happened. They divided 400 of us into platoons and had us march into our barracks. This was when they told me I was in charge of my entire platoon. So not only did I have to carry my pack on all the marches we did, but as the platoon leader, I also carried our flag.

We'd always get up around four in the morning and run, loaded down with our packs. We'd go to the beach and back, which was about eight miles. A couple of years before, the Marine Corps was doing the same thing that they did to us. Four men drowned on that trip. So they were trying to be a little softer. But still, I was there seven days before I could use the bathroom. Your body burns up every bit of waste.

After the beach run, we came back and did our PTO drills. Then we had breakfast and went through our day. One of the things we did regularly was an obstacle course—climbing robe, jumping over walls, stuff like that. Because I had always been an athlete, I was still in great shape. During the obstacle course, I pushed myself as hard as I could. I set a new record—a feat that was unheard of in the Marine Corps.

The gunnery sergeants used to like to hit us in the stomachs, and most guys would whimper and cry. But I would just laugh at them because I had already decided that they couldn't hurt me.

WHACK!

"Okay, what do you want?" I'd say.

I smoked at the time—a terrible habit—and the only way they let you smoke was for you to stand around in a circle with a bucket in the middle to put your ash in. You weren't allowed to talk. One day, one of the Marines started talking. The gunnery sergeant heard, came over, and brought us back to his lodge. Then he started beating *me.*

They never dared swing at our faces. As usual, I had a smile on my face the entire time—which I'm sure, in hindsight, was an antagonistic response.

"You're supposed to be in charge," the gunnery sergeant said between punches. "You take charge. You do whatever you need to do to be a leader."

The next day, we were in the smoking circle. One of the guys started talking. Despite my distaste for physical force as a means of enforcement, I walked over and hit the guy in the face. He fell directly to the ground. I mean, I didn't hold the state record for shot put for nothing.

I never had another problem with a Marine after that. Now, the guy I decked and his buddies threatened to kill me that night. But they were a bunch of chickens. I wasn't worried. They wouldn't have actually done anything.

After this incident, I was approached to join the Marine boxing team. The idea didn't appeal to me at all. I hated the idea of punching someone in the face as part of a sport. Violence of that sort has always made my stomach turn.

This was also about the same time that I took the ASVAB. No one was more surprised than me when I placed second. The guy who came in first was a brainiac, but he didn't make it through the Marine Corps because he couldn't understand logical things—only scientific facts. He flunked out, so I was the colonel's number-one guy.

When he asked me to be a pilot, I did what I always did—I asked him how much money that would earn me.

"If you become a pilot in Pensacola," he said, "you can make really good money. But you have to sign up for six years."

I'd already made a commitment to my boss that I'd be back in six months.

So I said, "What am I good at? Why are you giving me this opportunity?"

He said, "You figure things out."

And I said, "Okay, but I think I'm going to figure out how to make that much money and more by going home."

At the end of Marine Corps training, they give you an option to go to a few different camps. I chose Fort Benning because I wanted to be a parachutist. So next up was parachute school. The idea of jumping out of a plane was exciting to me.

I arrived in Fort Benning in Columbus, Georgia, along with the other Marine and Army parachutist hopefuls. Again, I chose to view the entire experience as a game. How long could I last? Because everybody around me was dropping like flies. It was hot as the dickens in Columbus, and as you might imagine, parachuting turned out to be a fairly dangerous pursuit.

The Marines are so crazy. They would jump out of the plane right behind you, maneuver over to you, and walk on the top of your chute, which makes your chute collapse, and you fall to the ground. You have to keep dodging them, making sure they're not above you. One guy fell and broke his back.

At the training drill, you take down these long lines attached to the pack, you raise your legs, and then you stand up on the bank of your landing location. Evidently, I was too heavy for my parachute, and I came in a little too hot. I ended up hitting the bank with my butt. I broke my coccyx—my tailbone—but I was there the next day, ready to jump again.

At some point, I ended up going to the doctor. I didn't want it to heal incorrectly and cause chronic pain down the road. The doctor said, "Well, there's only one way to fix a break like this." I won't tell you how to fix a coccyx break, but suffice it to say, I ended up fixing it myself.

I was never going to become a career military man. It just wasn't in my plans. I enjoyed the camaraderie and adventure, but I knew that lifestyle wouldn't make a free spirit like me happy for long. After my six-month training, I was honorably discharged and placed on reserve duty. The Marine Corps had been a wonderful experience, but now it was done. I returned to Tallahassee to resume my career at McDonald's.

Cliff was still at McDonald's. He and I had complementary skills, and we worked together like a finely tuned machine. He was a disciplined, organized person with a mind for numbers and an attitude that would fit in with corporate America. I was the marketer and motivator—I came up with ideas and got the staff excited to implement them. Although I also had a strong head for numbers, I left much of the finances in Cliff's capable hands.

Our talents were recognized differently at McDonald's. Cliff eventually moved to the corporate side of the company and ultimately became the Southeast Finance Manager. I was more of a ground employee—innovative, hardworking, and scrappy. My goal was to come up with ways to turn the Tallahassee branch into a success. I wasn't afraid to try new things.

Soon I was ready for the next step at McDonald's. Jerry, the owner of the store, loved to play golf. My time on the links at the Greenbrier was about to come in handy. One day Jerry and I were out on the fairway and I said, "Jerry, what's the busiest McDonald's in the world?"

Jerry responded, "Well, I think they are doing about $400,000." We were doing way less than that. The average McDonald's was grossing about $90,000 per year, and the profits were about 15 percent.

I said, "Jerry, I can make this McDonald's the busiest McDonald's in the world."

Jerry looked at me with a smirk. "Really," he said. "And what's in it for you?"

"If I can make us the busiest McDonald's in the world, I want a piece. I want a percentage of the gross."

Jerry laughed. He mulled over my proposal, clearly thinking of it as a golf wager. "I like it," he said finally. "Write something up."

So I went home and, on a yellow pad, wrote a couple of pages. The agreement stated that if I could get Jerry's McDonald's to gross anything over $200,000, I would receive 2 percent of the gross income. It was a safe bet for Jerry; the top McDonald's were grossing just over $120,000. There was no way I would be able to top that in a mostly quiet town like Tallahassee. And even if I were successful, he would be making more money off the franchise than ever before. Either way, he would win. It was a good business deal.

Jerry signed it, and I went to work.

As I look back, I'm sure Jerry saw me as an overly optimistic 21-year-old with his head in the clouds. What I was proposing was impossible, and he knew it. But Jerry was a motivator and wasn't going to dampen my spirits by pointing out the many ways I could fail. He stepped aside and let me try anyway.

And I gave it everything I had. I wrote a pamphlet called "76 Ways to Promote McDonald's" that would later become my Bible for marketing the restaurant to families, college students, children, and senior citizens. For example, one idea I had was a birthday club where you would give the birthday kid a free lunch, but he had to throw his party in your McDonald's. Everyone else had to pay—a cost that was still very affordable to them, while driving up sales for us.

I wanted the Tallahassee McDonald's to become *the* place for FSU students to hang out. In some promotions, I would target the frat boys. I knew they would eat more than anyone else, and my goal was to increase volume. I catered rush parties; I brought in marching bands. I heard that they were having trouble raising money for the Miss Florida 1960 pageant, so I let them do it in my parking lot. Once, I heard there were a bunch of bands coming to play at Doak Campbell Stadium. It gave me an idea.

I sent out promotional letters to all the bus drivers I could find in the Florida panhandle, telling them that whenever they brought a busload of customers, I would comp the driver's meal. It worked better than I could have dreamed. One day, I counted 25 busses in the parking lot. We had never been busier.

I was good at drawing a crowd, but that was only half the battle. I needed to make sure we could service every customer. In addition to marketing, I focused on making the concept of fast food even more convenient. With our spare operating funds, I bought a pink and white striped Jeep with fringe on the top. I put a sign on the back that said "McDonald's Delivery." I carted around hundreds of burgers, fries, and drinks to the campus on a daily basis. Everyone began to recognize the Jeep—it was an advertisement for itself.

I succeeded in creating buzz for the restaurant. But I also knew that buzz doesn't always translate into sales. So I made a gutsy move that could have made me famous—or gotten me fired. What it did, in my opinion, is change the way every McDonald's around the world would operate.

The old McDonald's layout had two little windows where you'd walk up, poke your head in, and order. Then you'd wait, get your food, and either eat in your car or take it home. There was no going inside for any reason—just the parking lot. I thought that was silly—we could do better. I decided to change the fundamental layout of the Tallahassee restaurant.

The way I remember it, I removed those two little windows, wiped out all the glass, and made it where I could put not two cash registers but four. I also installed something called a winter front—a sort of covered room attached to the face of the building so people could wait in line "inside" on a chilly December afternoon or a rainy evening. Now I could do a much greater volume, and people were standing in comfort. I took it a step further. I put concrete tables out front so people could sit down and eat their food while it was hot and fresh, without being stuck in their cars.

My strategy was shockingly simple, and I'm surprised no one had thought of it before. Or maybe they *had* thought of it but I was the only one foolish enough to try! Now, in addition to our great food, the Tallahassee McDonald's became known for its quick service. Multiple cash registers meant we collected the money sooner, and as our efficiency increased, so did our volume. Even with multiple points of sale running, there was often a line of customers that extended out toward the street. If I hadn't remodeled the front of the restaurant, we would have been overwhelmed. Our quality of service would have been compromised.

We were now drawing record crowds. Better yet, we were able to serve everyone great, affordable food both quickly and comfortably. I implemented all 76 promotions that first year.

And we became the number-one McDonald's in the world.

At the end of the year, I sat down with Jerry and showed him the numbers. We had surpassed my annual goal of $200,000. Our total volume for the year was a whopping $440,000. I would get 2 percent of the amount over $200,000—a bonus of $4,800 . That was nearly 40 times my weekly salary. The money thrilled me—I am human. But that wasn't what it was all about for me. I had come up with an idea and worked hard to implement it to success. I realized there were truly no limits to how successful I could be as long as I worked hard and created my own opportunities.

When our sales figures got back to McDonald's corporate offices, the board was blown away. We didn't usually see much of the corporate people. Tallahassee didn't have a large airport and was just out-of-the-way enough that they left us alone. But after a $440,000 year, we were on everyone's radar.

Sure, I received a nice bonus, but what I got that was more important was *noticed*. Ray Kroc, the owner of McDonald's, flew down in a small plane to see what the hell this Penrod kid was doing out in Tallahassee. He brought his president with him, and when they looked at the building, the president just went berserk.

"You're not allowed to change our building," he yelled. "It goes against franchise policy!"

Ray stayed for the day, watching and observing our store. Before he left, he said, "Don't listen to him. He doesn't have enough sense to design a matchbox. Do whatever you want." He saw that I was changing his business for the better.

Ray had put a lot of trust in me, and I didn't want to violate it. Although some of my ideas were radical, they all had a purpose. Every move I made was calculated to increase volume and profitability. I had seen what Ray was able to achieve and wanted to duplicate it someday. I instinctively knew that I had to nurture my relationship with him and make sure he was pleased with my performance.

Jerry came to me one day with a proposal. He and Ray played a lot of golf together. They'd decided it was time for Jerry to expand his McDonald's operations to Fort Lauderdale. It was his favorite part of the country—he and Ray Kroc had spent countless hours playing golf in the area, plus Ray had a home there.

In the early 1960s, South Florida was one of the fastest growing areas of America. Jerry saw it as a way to make easy money, especially by putting me in charge of managing the restaurant. He asked if I would be willing to head to South Florida to open up a new store. I jumped at the chance. At the age of 25, I would return to South Florida, where I had grown up. It felt like coming home.

My brother Bob was in the Marines and had just gotten out. He was working with the survey team in the Florida Everglades. I said, "Bob, why don't you come and work with me?" He came, and I had a little backup. Of course, he was a rough and tumble kid. So I made him be the janitor for the first year as a trial run—to see how he did in the food-service industry. After the first year, I promoted Bob to second-in-command. I finally had someone I could depend on.

My life was good. I enjoyed my work. I was making money. But believe it or not, I was already craving a new adventure.

One weekend I went to the Miami boat show. I saw this little sailboat that I just loved the look of—it was only 31-feet long. I'd never sailed before, but I wasn't intimidated by the idea of giving it a shot.

I told the sales guy, "I'll take that boat. How soon can you put it in the water?"

"Tomorrow," he said. I was probably his easiest sale of the entire event!

I spent a day getting ready, invited two friends, and then packed up the sailboat—which we called *BIG MAC*—and sailed it to the Bahamas. The two guys with me had sailing experience, but none of us were knowledgeable enough to be out alone. Besides, they were older and relying on me to be the muscle of the operation.

I don't know why, but I chose to start this excursion at night. In the distance, I started to make out a form in the water. It was a tree. *No problem*, I thought, *I'll just steer us around it.* We were moving slowly, so I sailed us around safely and hoped that was our last bit of excitement before we arrived at our destination.

But that's not what happened.

I heard this loud rumble in the water. Not knowing what it was, I searched the black distance ahead of us. Then, finally, lights came into view. It was another boat. Actually, *boat* is not even a good word to describe what I saw in front of me. It was a tug boat pulling a mountainous bar ge. And the barge was probably ten stories high, full of cargo.

I was in between the tug and the barge. I suddenly realized that the barge—that looked more like a condominium—was coming right at us.

I was in a panic at that point, my sails luffing—meaning, the sales are just fluttering—and I'm watching this thing get closer and closer. And it was gigantic. After the barge passed, it sucked me in. I was out of control, going into the back of the barge, my sail being so much lower than the top. There was no way the guy running it would even know I was there. So I hit the back of the barge, breaking my spar off. The collision was so forceful that it pushed my sailboat back far enough to give me the chance to get the sails out in time and manage to turn it around missing another collision with the barge which it could had been the end of me.

It motored right on, never even realizing I'd been there.

My passengers were in a state of absolute terror. Seriously—they were almost dead. One guy almost had a heart attack. I quickly got us to safety and got my new boat repaired. I figured I'd take a few sailing lessons before I attempted another journey. But, on the bright side, we did catch a *huge* amount of fish!

Time passed quickly during these years. I met someone and got married. The record-breaking volume at our McDonald's continued, but there were issues that ran far deeper than the sale of hamburgers.

Segregation was in full force throughout the South. The idea of "separate but equal" was still on everyone's mind. Many restaurants and stores had signs in their front window that read "We Have the Right to Refuse Service to Anyone."

These signs were a thinly disguised way to deny service to Black customers—an idea that was unacceptable to me. As the South began to integrate, there were demonstrations throughout Tallahassee. Riots broke out daily. Buildings were lit on fire. At one point, we had to usher the McDonald's staff to the basement for their own safety. We spent many nights on the roof of that McDonald's with guns, trying to protect our staff and our store.

I hated the chaos of that period. I have always believed that people should be judged by their character and actions, not by the color of their skin. All these years later, I still believe the same thing.

Besides, even in the midst of political and social upheaval, this was the start of another new adventure.

A MAN OF PRINCIPLES

"Don't ever be afraid to be innovative. People are often reluctant to try some-thing new because it hasn't been done before. A lot of it comes down to timing. A bad idea now may turn into a good idea later. You'll never know for sure until you try."

—JACK

I didn't have a lot of money when I returned to South Florida. I knew there was a lot of hard work ahead of me, but I didn't mind. It was a new challenge, and Fort Lauderdale seemed like a land of opportunity for me. I had done well in Tallahassee, and I planned to duplicate that success in a more vibrant part of the state.

We opened the Fort Lauderdale store, and we were off. I was putting in the hours too—I worked from open to close every day. I never minded though. I didn't trust anyone as much as I trusted myself. I've always known that success doesn't just fall in your lap. You have to chase it and earn it.

Then I got the phone call that would change everything. Jerry, the owner, was very sick. He wasn't expected to make it. He said,

"Will you come back to the Tallahassee store? I want to talk about giving you the Fort Lauderdale operation."

I couldn't just pack up and leave the Fort Lauderdale McDonald's. I was still doing so much of the work myself to get us off the ground. It couldn't function without me yet. I said, "Give me a week, and I'll be there."

But while I was making arrangements to head back north, Jerry passed away.

After the funeral, there were conversations about the fate of Jerry's holdings. His widow said she disagreed with the maneuver—she said she wasn't going to give me the Fort Lauderdale store after all.

I said, "I'm a man of principle, Mrs. Olson. And going back on your husband's word goes against my values. I can't work for you anymore." I couldn't just walk away from the store and leave her stranded, but I determined to make arrangements to move on from the Fort Lauderdale McDonald's as soon as it was appropriate.

Ray Croc heard what had transpired between Jerry and me, and he gave me a call. He had talked his golf buddy Harold Hill into coming to Fort Lauderdale to meet with me. By that point I certainly had the skills to succeed, but I wouldn't be able to come up with the money I would need to buy into the business. Harold and I met. We talked about how we could become partners.

But this time the terms needed to be different. I wasn't going to break my back again to make someone else rich. I needed to come up with a deal for Harold—something that would make us both happy.

That's one of the most important lessons I've learned in business—the best negotiations never leave one party feeling cheated or shortchanged. A good deal—a truly successful agreement—will benefit both parties. When both sides are happy, they will be motivated to execute their end of the bargain. But if one side feels duped, they will consciously or unconsciously sabotage the deal. I didn't want that to happen with Harold Hill. The right deal would make us both a lot of money. The wrong one would result in bitterness and hurt feelings. Because we didn't know each other very well, we needed to have an exit strategy in case our partnership didn't work out.

I met with Harold, and he was willing to work with me. He asked me what I wanted.

"I want you to let me do my thing," I replied. Harold agreed and allowed me to handle things however I saw fit. Ray must have told him about my history with the company because Harold trusted me from the beginning.

I made a promise to Harold: we would open two restaurants. Eventually we'd decide which was the better-performing store. That one I'd teach his son-in-law how to run, and Harold would keep it. The lower-performing store would become mine. It seemed like a good plan to me because I was confident in my abilities to grow a McDonald's. I had done it before, and I was excited to do it again. Harold liked the deal. He agreed to the terms, and we got to work.

The next year was a blur. I immersed myself in my job, handling every detail of the management. I worked from open to close seven days a week. I focused on increasing our volume and streamlining the business. As promised, we had two Fort Lauderdale locations: one on Commercial Boulevard and another one on Sunrise Boulevard. As the year progressed, the Commercial Boulevard location started to take off. The volume wasn't record-breaking, but it was strong. We turned a tidy profit each month.

I ate a *lot* of McDonald's. I never go to the doctor—I've never been sick—but when I did finally go in for a physical, he said, "You have so much grease in you. We're gonna have to feed you charcoal to get it out." When you work open to close, there's no way around eating a lot of cheeseburgers. And there's the fries too. And the fish sandwich came along during this time—it was delicious, but still pretty greasy. I might as well have been sipping from the grease pit! But man, it was a great burger. There was nothing else to eat there. I wouldn't let any of my staff bring in outside food, so I didn't bring in outside food.

I took all my meals at my desk—it was a standup desk in a little office I had in the back. It was the only time I used that desk. I found that most managers of McDonald's would get on a little bit of a power trip and sit in their offices all day. Not me. I stayed out front with my customers and staff. I have had probably 500,000 employees throughout all my businesses and I've made it my mission to know them all. I had more than a few go on to be successful in their own right.

In fact, a few years ago my wife, Lucia, went in to have a small procedure done on her toe. The doctor doing the procedure looked at me funny and said, "Are you Jack Penrod?"

"Depends . . . who's asking?" I teased.

She laughed. "I used to work for you. You were the best boss I've ever had."

As a franchise owner, I realized that if I wanted my stores to be the best, it was up to me to set the pace for everything. I had to do the accounting, the marketing, the hiring, and the training. But I didn't mind. I knew my time was the most important investment I could make into my stores. I would bring in young people, and I would help them master one skill at a time. For example, in one day, I'd teach them how to make the perfect batch of French fries. They would learn how to peel the potato, blanch the potato, fry it, cook it, box it, and sell it. Same with hamburgers; same with milkshakes. I divided it up into categories.

Eventually I learned that retirees made some of my best employees. A McDonald's is busiest at lunchtime, say, eleven to two. I would hire these senior citizens—some of them in their eighties—and all they did was make milkshakes. Or fries. Or drinks. Or whatever singular skill I wanted them to focus on. They were really good at it too. They enjoyed having somewhere to be during the day and their work supplemented their Social Security.

As our volume increased, I searched for ways to improve efficiency and lower overhead. When I realized that I couldn't cut the costs of my electric, water, or insurance bills, I quickly learned the importance of letting certain things go. I simply paid them and focused on the costs I could change. I worked hard to control the money spent on my food, drinks, and, most of all, labor.

Some of the employees needed some extra training in basic social skills. We taught general manners about grooming and how to talk to people. This was usually the first job these people had ever had! If their work habits were strong, I was happy to teach them the rest.

Perhaps my most successful strategy was choosing the right food suppliers. Instead of shopping around for the cheapest options, I found a supplier who would give me 90 days to pay for my ingredients. It was like having a short-term loan.

It wasn't long before my first franchise started doing well. Really well. Ray gave me a call and said, "Do you want to expand?"

I said, "Sure."

So I opened the second store, and then the third one. All the other McDonald's franchisees started complaining because I was getting all new products.

Ray called me again. He said, "Do you have any family?"

I said, "You have no idea. I've got a whole bunch of 'em."

I brought in my brother Chuck, and they gave me a couple more stores. I brought in my brother Bob—even more stores. I brought in my brother-in-law. As they would come into the business, I'd give them 10 percent ownership. Then I taught them everything I knew about being a manager. They went on to be very wealthy people in the McDonald's world because when I started, there were only 285 franchises; now there are close to 40,000.

I worked seven days a week for seven years straight, without a single day off. But at the end of the seven years, I was the owner of 16 McDonald's stores. We were extremely busy. I bought a little building, an old house, and I made it our group's central office. We would meet there every morning, talk through our day, strategize, and then everyone would go to work.

After I built my third McDonald's, I took a careful look at my finances. I knew I was becoming rich, but I wanted to know the bottom line. It was 1968 and I was nearing 30; I wanted to see how rich I was. The answer surprised me. I was worth more than a million dollars. I had made it. The promise I had made to my mother was fulfilled.

I had been taking care of her for years, after all. I had paid off her house several years earlier. But now I was a *millionaire*. Flashes of memories rushed through my mind: Mother clipping coupons and counting pennies; Mother skipping meals so we could eat; Mother rushing home to change clothes before she went to her second or third job of the day. She had sacrificed her entire life for us kids. She never had to worry about money again. My brothers and I would provide for her for the rest of her life.

Everything about my career was working out perfectly. Everyone knew about McDonald's—especially ours. We packed each restaurant during the lunch and dinner rushes.

My family continued to grow. My daughter Michelle was born in 1965, Tracey came along in 1967, and Michael in 1969. I was now the father of three. I felt very blessed to take care of them in a way that my parents were unable to provide for me.

So I did what any business-minded man would do—I diversified by investing in another company. I bought a meat-packing operation.

We packed our meat in Tampa, and I would personally pick it up and deliver it during the night. As an owner of a restaurant, I didn't want those big trucks in my parking lot during the day, and I wanted to show my customers the same respect. My company delivered to most of the McDonald's in South Florida. Then, as we grew, it took one hassle out of running the business by keeping up with inventory.

It was the same with my landscaping. I was having trouble finding the kind of plants I wanted for our stores' landscaping. I found a lady who owned a beautiful restaurant that she'd been landscaping and growing plants at for years. It was only five acres, but it was a fine five. So we named it "Granny's Garden," and I landscaped all of my McDonald's using her plants. One of my McDonald's gardens even won a landscaping award from the city!

In the mid 1960s I got my pilot's license and a small plane to get around on to visit all my McDonald's stores. I was missing the Keys so much that I also decided to get a commercial fishing license to set traps for lobster. But first I had to learn how to build the lobster traps. I met a friend in the Bahamas who showed me how to do it.

The traps had to be dipped in diesel because that's what attracts the lobsters. I had a license to have a hundred traps, so it was quite an ordeal to get them built. I then had to put them in my small boat and make sure the ropes and buoys were attached correctly before I started placing my traps along a line in shallow water.

I had arranged with a friend to keep my boat on a trailer, so I would fly into Marathon, grab the boat, put it in the water, and pull my traps. I flew into Marathon every couple of weeks, and then I'd take my catch to Key's Fishery, where they would process it all. I sold most of the lobsters to them, actually. And the rest I ate or gave to my friends—which meant I had many happy friends. I really enjoyed the entire process until one Marathon trip. I was pulling up the traps and I felt a searing pain in my right arm. Turns out, most people with traps use machinery to pull them up, not muscle. And I had torn mine. Thus, my lobstering days were over.

In time, I bought a nicer house, fancy cars, and any toy that I wanted. Although I was enormously busy, I tried to spend as much time with my children as possible; I had seen the pitfalls of children who grew up with hardworking parents, and I tried to avoid them with my kids.

In the late 1960s, I chartered a sailboat and headed 200 miles east to the Bahamas. I quickly fell in love with being on the open water, and the Bahamas seemed like a wonderful vacation retreat. My friend Stan Smoker approached me with the idea of buying Scotland Cay, a private island in the Bahamas. It was ready-made for a resort, with 15 miles of roads and a gravel runway for seaplanes.

The idea of owning a private island was fascinating. What seemed like an impossible dream was suddenly a feasible plan. Stan had assembled five businessmen to go in together on purchasing the island, but each one had his own financial strains. One by one, everyone else dropped out of the deal, leaving Stan and me as the only ones making payments on the island. It had no power or running water yet. Those amenities would come later. To me, it was a tropical paradise.

We began selling lots on the island for $20,000 each, back in the late '60s and early '70s. Those lots are now worth about $400,000 each.

A homeowner's association formed and it became a deed-restricted community. But one thing was nonnegotiable for me—I would keep the southernmost part of the island, and there I would eventually build a home that would be my respite from the craziness of the world of Mc-Donald's. I initially built a home with a 24- by 24-foot grand room and one bedroom. As the years went by, I built guest cottages with the input of my family and added 13 bedrooms over the next 20 years.

While Scotland Cay was initially a business investment, it soon played a vital role in my own sanity and wellbeing. I would fly to the island on Fridays to clear my head. As I would draw closer to the island, I would feel the stress evaporate. I wouldn't pack any food for my Bahamas trip. That would take away the thrill of it. Instead, I would go spear fishing. I never went hungry.

I have some wonderful memories of my kids and me at Scotland Cay. Years ago, I decided to put a little house on the island. I did it ecologically. I didn't want electricity there, so I put in gas lines instead, getting as many gas-run appliances as possible. I put a cistern under the house, and I hand-pumped water to the holding tank on top that held a couple hundred gallons of water. And the kids knew that when we ran out of water, that's all they had for the day.

I would get up in the morning and say, "Okay, what do you want to eat? Lobster? Shrimp?" It would be no longer than a half hour in a kayak before I had an entire slew of fresh food for us to cook and eat. I had these big cooking pots that I would fill with peanut oil. I'd build a fire out in front of the house and make the most delicious food you've ever tasted.

My mom gave me a recipe for cream of fish soup, where you cut fish into small squares, bread it, and drop it in. It's better than anything you can buy in a restaurant—and probably the reason I have so much mercury in my system.

But after a relaxing weekend at Scotland Cay, I'd feel the familiar pressure build back up in my body. Running so many McDonald's restaurants was taking its toll on me. I didn't dread returning to work, but my mind would start thinking of all the things that were left to do.

As a young man, I was most afraid of my body giving out—that I would find myself too physically exhausted to work. But when I began working at McDonald's, I realized that bodily fatigue wasn't the worst thing that could happen—mental and spiritual exhaustion are far more dangerous. The weekends at Scotland Cay were the best way for me to calm and rejuvenate myself. It was the best place for me to find respite from the storms that came with my responsibility.

And the storms were just beginning.

TAKING STOCK

"A person can learn a lot from working at a fast-food restaurant. A good employee will learn a lot of different skills—from management to people skills. You don't have to work in fast-food forever, but you will be able to develop skills that will last you a lifetime."

—JACK

Despite my accomplishments at McDonald's, not everyone was a fan of my way of doing things. I was producing phenomenal numbers and I had neither the time nor the energy to entertain baseless criticism of my work. My success had made me a highly visible target. I occasionally found my management style colliding with other people within the McDonald's corporation. When we disagreed, things could get heated.

Many people envied my close relationship with Ray Kroc. From my first interaction with him, we clicked. I looked to him as a mentor and father figure, and I believe he was happy to take on that role. When colleagues grew jealous, they did whatever they could to discredit me.

If I had to choose someone who liked me the *least,* that would be Fred Turner, another fast-rising star in the McDonald's Corporation. Fred was a forceful, type-A manager with cold blue eyes and a combover on his bald head. He was ambitious and smart, with an attention to detail that was both his biggest asset and his biggest liability. Fred was the president of the company—the same president who did *not* appreciate my changing the structure of the Tallahassee store years prior.

Fred began his fast-food career in 1956, when he was just 23 years old. He had been discharged from the U.S. Army and found his niche as a McDonald's grill operator. He was a good worker, and he quickly rose through the ranks of the company. By 1958, he had been named operations vice president, when McDonald's only had 34 employees. Fred would be a lifer at the McDonald's corporation; he didn't have the vision of starting his own place. His path to success would be moving up the corporate ladder.

Fred was a stickler for the minutiae, and he hated any deviation from his strict, unbending guidelines. He even decreed that all our hamburgers needed to be "precisely .28 inches thick" and that "exactly ten patties had to be formed from each pound of beef." He concentrated on rigid uniformity. Some of his guidelines made sense. His motto was "Quality, Service, and Cleanliness," and he wanted to make sure that customers' experience were consistent everywhere in the world.

But to me, some of his guidelines were rules for the sake of having rules, with little thought behind them. His corporatism was an enemy to my innovation. He was like a computer—if anything deviated from his precise specifications, he would immediately reject it. He was not a fan of the freewheeling Penrod brothers in South Florida, despite the fact that we were making a lot of money for the corporation.

Fred was on the upwardly mobile track at McDonald's. By 1967, he became the executive vice president. In 1968, he was promoted to president and chief administrative officer. He was gunning for Ray's position as chairman. I knew that when Ray eventually stepped aside, I would have a formidable adversary in Fred.

But I tried not to worry about him. I certainly didn't take his criticisms of our group personally. Not everyone is going to like you in business, especially when you're making more money that they are. While Fred rose through the ranks, I was having remarkable successes of my own in South Florida. I came up with my own criteria for running my franchise and we were experiencing unprecedented growth. I instituted skills tests for all employees. I chose star staff members from each location and promoted them into trainers. One of my strengths has always been personnel motivation, and I worked hard to keep them happy.

Instinctively, I knew that I couldn't grow employees and keep them in the same position forever. They had to see an upward trajectory to their careers. That sense of achievement and promise of advancement would keep them loyal. I never had to hire managers from the outside because I always had a stable of qualified employees ready to go. When I would open a new location, I would promote from within. I made it a point to reward hard work and competence with more responsibility—and more compensation. Money talks a lot louder than words.

On an ordinary afternoon in 1973, I corralled 16 managers and 4 supervisors into our company office for a regular business meeting. My managers were young, ambitious, and eager to please—and I knew they would be forever loyal with the right motivation. My brother, Bob and I began the meeting like we always did, by talking about the vision of McDonald's and our sales goals for the next quarter. Then, without warning, I threw 20 sets of car keys out on the conference table.

"Step outside and see what I got," I told them.

When the managers stepped into the parking lot, they saw 20 brand-new Pontiacs sitting in neat rows. As the men stared at the cars, their mouths hanging open, I spoke up loudly. "These cars are yours as long as you keep working here. I hope you like them."

As the gift sank in, the managers crowded around me. I was showered with handshakes and hugs—and I was genuinely glad I could do something nice for them. Now that they were suddenly driving vehicles far beyond the reach of most young men their age, I knew they would remain motivated and loyal. And all it cost me was a small car payment each month.

The menu was expanding. Some of the locations now had children's play areas. Perhaps one of the most important things we did in the 1970s was the creation of co-op advertising. At the time, McDonald's-at-large didn't have the budget to do TV commercials. Almost every home in America had a television at this point, and if you weren't doing TV commercials, you were missing out on a huge opportunity.

So all of the McDonald's operators would get together nationwide and chip in 1 percent of our sales for advertising. Not only did the aggressive marketing campaign boost sales tremendously, but it seared McDonald's into the national consciousness. These were the days of Ronald McDonald and catchy jingles.

Within a few years, my group doubled, then tripled our profits, because all of a sudden, we're the people on TV—the Penrods of South Florida. McDonald's had become the benchmark for brand development. It was more than a household name—it became an American icon.

In Dade and Broward counties, we formed our own co-op with the same business model. I became president of the co-op for several years and worked closely with local radio, newspaper, and television marketing. As I brainstormed commercial ideas, I wondered aloud how many hamburgers we had sold. I somehow figured out that if you were to put our hamburgers end to end, they'd stretch around the equator of the world. That idea took off and soon all the McDonald's were promoting how many hamburgers they had ever sold.

While I always stood behind the quality of our product at McDonald's, there was a lesson in the ad campaign—people gravitate to things that are popular. By highlighting how many people loved eating McDonald's hamburgers, we managed to make them even more desirable to the general public. No one wanted to be the only one who didn't eat at McDonald's.

Our franchise was a family business. My brothers were supervisors and money was pouring in. In 1973, I had one of the most significant markers in my career. At the age of 34, I had begun earning more than $1 million per year. Although I had promised my mother that I would someday be a millionaire, I don't think I ever considered that I might make that amount annually. I was flying high.

But something had started to change. When McDonald's was young, it felt like a family business. Everyone knew everyone else, and there was an easy camaraderie between franchisees and the corporate office. But as the company grew, the family vibe began to fade away. The corporation hired field representatives to watch over franchises. They were often young kids directly out of college. Their job was to tell me how to run my operation, regardless of the fact that they had never once worked in the industry. Suddenly, working at McDonald's became a lot less fun.

Generally, I have always resisted people who substitute their education for practical experience. I am a big fan of college; I believe higher education is the right step for many people to take. But that education can't out-perform real-world experience. I have never asked anyone to do something that I wouldn't do (except maybe my brother Bob). These field representatives had no such conviction, and their presence in the stores was met with resistance and resentment.

Despite the more corporate feel of McDonald's, things were becoming more financially rewarding. In 1974, I opened eleven new McDonald's locations in South Florida. While opening a restaurant per month sounds exciting, I was gripped by a growing discontentment. I stopped enjoying the thrill of the hunt. The challenge was gone, and it felt like I was simply going through the motions.

By the mid 1970s, I was getting bored, both in my personal and professional life. I stopped going to meetings. Instead of focusing on my businesses, my mind was everywhere else. I was often on the golf course, playing 36 holes per day. It was a retirement of sorts, where I could enjoy my time away from the office. My complacency made me feel guilty, like I was checking out of my life.

I decided that I needed some sort of new challenge.

Once I learned to fly, I realized that I'm not a pilot who loves to get up in the air and fly around. But I *do* love the ability to get to places very quickly—especially the American West. I started taking my children out there when they were just babies. We'd stay for weeks at a time in the summer. But in the fall, I'd return with my brothers. I would take all of them to a hunting lodge in Jackson, Wyoming. We'd go out on horseback and hunt for elk and deer, staying ten days at a time.

I had this urge to go out into the woods alone to see how I fared living off the land. I found a primitive area in Idaho near a town named McCall that was about a hundred miles square. I flew my aircraft into Chamberlain Basin, an air strip with about a 10,000-foot elevation in the middle of absolutely nowhere.

As I said, I had decided to live off the land, so I didn't bring any food with me. I loaded a backpack with the necessary supplies and hiked about five miles to an area called Moose Jaw Meadow. As I started hiking, there was a light rain that quickly turned into snow. About two hours later, I stopped and started to set up my camp.

The first thing I did was build a fire. As soon as I gained visibility, I saw a pair of eyes glowing in the distance. And they were looking straight at me. Slowly, a huge puma crept toward my camp. I stayed calm—probably because I was too cold, wet, and tired to care. I continued to set up camp, but I kept a close eye on my new friend.

That night I did not sleep very well. I could see the puma's gaze on me from the edge of the tree line, circling my camp around and around. So I stayed awake and alert all night. That puma never stopped moving. I imagine he didn't want to come near the fire— but he sure wanted to eat. As daylight dawned, I could hear him moving as he went toward the elk in the distance. I'm sure he was disappointed in his breakfast after a night spent craving human flesh.

Later that day, I found a forest ranger and told him about my encounter. He said that I should have killed the puma. He reported that there had been something going on with the mountain cats in the area. He looked at me like I was foolish, but I felt good about my choice. I don't like killing things I don't plan on eating.

The next day I was walking a trail cut out by these rangers when all of a sudden a bear jumped out in the path in front of me. Being a Marine, my knee-jerk reaction was to pull out my gun and shoot him. And I hit him right in the head.

There I was, thinking, *What in the hell am I going to do with this thing now?* I couldn't just leave him there, so I went over and I started opening him, quartering him, because now I've got to take him to the airport out of respect for the loss of his life.

When I took his skull to the taxidermist, he said, "Where did you shoot this bear?"

"In the head," I told him.

The taxidermist shook his head. "No, you didn't. There's no hole in this skull. You must have just injured him when you shot the gun. Jack, I'm afraid you didn't kill him until you cut him up."

I'd walk along the trails and look for my next meal. There were these birds called fool's hens, which are really just grouse, that would line up on tree branches. They were easy to pick off one by one because they didn't fly away once you fired your gun. So I always had plenty to eat.

During these extended trips by myself, I became so in tune with nature and my environment that I could actually smell what kind of animal was coming up over the hill toward me. Anyway, on that first trip, I stayed alive by eating squirrel and grouse for two weeks. When I came home with the bear meat, I mixed the bear meat with a little pork, rolled it into balls, and invited my friends over to taste a little bear. I called it a "Bear Ball" party, but really, you couldn't taste any bear at all.

Personally, things weren't going well at home either. I went through a divorce. "Write down what you want and it's yours," I said. I've never understood husbands and fathers who try to give their ex-spouse the least amount of money and resources possible.

After the divorce, I bought a home two blocks away, and I bought my son a boat. He was able to come by canal to my house any time he wanted.

Being so close, I was still the main disciplinarian. I'd get a call that one of the kids had done something and I needed to come over right away and handle it.

So I'd take the offending kid upstairs in the house and I'd turn them over my knee. But instead of spanking their bottoms like I was expected to, I'd just smack my hands together.

"You better start crying," I'd whisper.

I was never very good at the corporal punishment thing.

In late 1975, I was on a plane with Fred Turner on our way back from giving a speech in Hawaii. I stood up on the plane and started pouring myself some coffee. I saw Fred looking at me with an unhappy face. "Every time Ray comes home from his winter holiday, do you know what he wants to talk about?"

"What?" I asked, knowing this was not a good start to the conversation.

"Jack's doing this, and Jack's doing that," he said. "I just can't put up with it anymore."

"What do you want me to do?" I asked. "When I know Ray's in town, I make sure my stores are extra clean and well-staffed. I'm not going to stop being a good McDonald's guy for the sake of your ego, Fred."

"Jack," he sighed heavily, "do you have any idea how hard you make my job?"

"I run a good place, Fred," I said. "I make a lot of money—not just for myself, but for the entire McDonald's corporation."

"But the way you do it makes my life harder," he said.

I hadn't realized part of my job description was to remove obstacles from Fred Turner's professional journey. I probably said as much because Fred leaded toward me and said, "Do you think you could do my job any better than I do it?"

That was the wrong question to ask a guy like me because I had a proven track record and a lot of confidence. I looked him in the eye. "Yes," I said with certainty. "I could definitely do your job better."

By this point, Fred was furious. He started yelling. I remember my accountant, Peter Bonitatibus, was with me, and the poor guy looked terrified. Fred did seem a little unhinged, so I don't blame him.

"I want you out! I want you OUT!" Fred hollered.

I knew this day would come—the day when the emotional cost of dealing with Fred would outweigh the financial profits. I had no desire to work in a company whose leadership was as shortsighted as Fred Turner's. Besides, I'd broken my back for the company. I'd gone through enough.

"Buy me out if you want me gone," I said. "Just name a price."

Fred started at $3 million, but that wasn't nearly enough for me. I laughed at him and got off the plane. But I knew that wasn't the last I'd hear from Fred.

That plane ride signaled the end of my personal investment in McDonald's. I stopped all meetings and trainings. I was running the marketing department for all of South Florida, and I simply backed off.

The next number Fred came back with was $5 million. I said no.

Then he came back at $6 million. Still not enough.

See, I knew they weren't buying my franchise. It was bigger than that. By 1975, McDonald's had the clout to open restaurants anywhere they wanted to. They were buying my team of people—my managers, supervisors, and regular employees. Fred knew that I had found a formula that worked, and he wanted to buy it.

When they finally got to $10 million for all my McDonald's stores and staff, I said yes. "But I don't just want cash," I told them. "I want stock in the company too."

When Fred first started talking to me about buying me out, the price of McDonald's shares were $42 each. I wanted mine to be pegged at $42. Of course they yelled and screamed, but eventually they said yes. For me, I understood the process. If they bought my company that was making a million a year, it was worth 10 million to them on the books. If you take my million and add it to theirs, the stock would inevitably go up.

I was right. By the time I finally got my stock, it wasn't at $42 a share—it was at $65. So my value was well over $10 million, which in today's dollars is about a $55 million net worth.

I remember entering the building for the closing of our deal. They had about twelve accountants and lawyers. I showed up with my attorney and my brother Bob. It was a lot like the movies—we were all sitting at this big, long conference room table, everybody acting really stoic and serious. At one point, one of the attorneys addressed Bob and asked him a question.

Bob sort of shrugged. "You're going to have to ask Jack," he said. "He's the one who graduated high school. I never did."

I laughed. Bob would do well in this deal too, coming out wealthier than maybe all the highly educated and well-dressed attorneys combined. And he didn't even have a high school diploma.

The poor kid with no pedigree to speak of and his illiterate brother got everything they wanted in the boardroom that day. I got every single thing I wanted.

That day on the plane, I watched Fred's anger increase. I became more and more amused. By the time the dust settled, I had sold my McDonald's franchises back to the company for well over three times what they had initially offered me. It wasn't a bad deal. Those stores would continue to bring in high-grossing revenues. Like me or not, I'd left my mark on the franchise. I was proud of the work I'd done.

Now I was wealthier than I'd ever been, and I was only 36 years old. I looked toward my next adventure. Besides, those fancy attorneys had missed an important detail in our contract negotiations. They forgot to add a noncompete clause.

BANKRUPT

"I know that people would say I lost everything, but I really didn't. I may have lost some money, but I didn't lose my intelligence. I didn't lose my sense of adventure. I didn't lose my ambition. If anything, I became more determined to succeed and to become a bigger success than I had ever been before. What I lost was easy to replace. What I kept was priceless."

—JACK

My departure from McDonald's sent shockwaves throughout the entire company. I had been instrumental in McDonald's growth, and everyone knew it—especially Ray Kroc. After I decided to leave the company, he came to my office and cried. He begged me to stay. He was more than just a boss; we had become very good friends over the last decade, and I would always appreciate how much he had trusted me and mentored me.

Unfortunately, there was an unintended consequence of my decision to leave. Ray was so wrapped up with McDonald's that he couldn't maintain friendships outside the company. We never spoke again after I left. I missed being able to talk with him, but I always admired what he was able to achieve and how much he had influenced me.

But after being at the company for more than 15 years, I knew it was time for me to move on and seek new opportunities. I didn't want to become stagnant. Besides, Fred wasn't going anywhere. And I don't make it a habit of partnering with people who are counting on my eventual failure.

My goal had always been to create something that would outlast my life. I wanted to build something that would provide for my family for generations to come—something I could hand off to them one day. As wonderful as my time at McDonald's had been, I was unlikely to build something that long-lasting while I worked for someone else—and even less likely to build something transferable.

I was now in my mid thirties—the time was right to build something permanent. I had learned some lessons, made some mistakes, and done more than a few things right. I thought it would be impossible for me to fail at whatever came next, right?

The news of my buyout soon spread beyond the borders of McDonald's and throughout the fast-food industry. The day after I signed the paperwork, I got a call from Jack Massy, the owner of the KFC franchise in California. Mr. Massy asked me to partner with him to grow Wendy's. I would be put in charge of the California region during the mid '70s. It would be an opportunity to make a lot of money while doing many of the same things I had done in the past. The job was mine if I wanted it.

On the one hand, it was an intriguing proposition. Wendy's had experienced phenomenal growth in the early 1970s. The first restaurant had opened in my hometown of Columbus just six years earlier. It caught on quickly, leading to many more restaurants throughout Ohio, Pennsylvania, and Indiana. The first franchise had been sold in 1973 and had done very well. When I got the offer, Wendy's was nearing 500 locations nationwide—a stunning number for a restaurant that was just six years old.

In many ways, 1975 Wendy's reminded me of McDonald's in 1960. In fact, the national media was saying Wendy's might topple McDonald's from its dominance in the fast-food market. Jack Massy was giving me the opportunity to grow along with Wendy's. I would be overseeing the country's fastest-growing restaurant in a burgeoning region of America. I had to consider his offer.

I had enough money from the McDonald's buyout that I could carefully and methodically plan my next step. I mulled over Mr. Massy's proposition. And I had some serious reservations. Chief among those was the location. Since the work would take me to the West Coast, I would have to move away from my children. I also knew working at Wendy's would likely be a continuation of what I had done for the past decade and a half. I would be working for someone else, not myself. While I knew I could make a lot of money—perhaps even more than I had made at McDonald's—I was ready to build something of my own. I appreciated the offer, but ultimately decided to turn Jack Massy down. I never regretted the decision.

It's a common mistake to make career choices based on money rather than passion. Given the choice between two opportunities, money should not always be the primary consideration. When people are happy with their work, they tend to do a better job—and the money usually follows.

If I had really needed the cash, I might have seriously considered taking the offer. But I was wealthy now. I had the luxury of taking my time to plot out what I wanted to do next. I was not motivated by financial gain. Instead of chasing a higher paycheck, I decided to pursue new adventures and life experience. I didn't want to do something that I would eventually grow to regret solely because it would make me richer than I already was. I decided to pursue happiness instead.

During this period of contemplation, I flew to Hawaii on a week-long vacation with my then-girlfriend, Christine . We stayed at the Royal Hawaiian Hotel, at the time a luxurious beachfront resort with an upscale clientele. The décor was typical 1970s Hawaii—brightly colored floral linens, purple and lavender wall prints, and bamboo furniture. It was a modern, attractive, exotic look. I thought it was a look that would catch the eye of potential customers in a new venture.

On my way back home from the trip, I stopped by the airport gift shop to pick up a few things for the kids. One of the things I bought was a teddy bear that had a tag on it that read "I wuv you." That was it—*Wuv.* I thought *WUV's* would be a warm, family-friendly name that everyone would grow to *love.*

I put everything together in my head. This would be my next multimillion-dollar idea. When I returned to Florida on May 23,

1975, I incorporated WUV's International. I was going back into the fast-food business, this time as the sole owner and operator. The décor would be purple and white—based on the prints that I saw in the Aloha State.

In retrospect, the warning signs that I was moving too quickly were glaringly obvious, but I couldn't see them at the time. I forged ahead—blindly unaware that everything about the marketing concept was wrong. The name was ridiculous. It was complete nonsense, but I didn't think it was important. After all, I reasoned, if Kleenex could create a brand based on a name that didn't mean anything, why couldn't I?

The colors also had mixed connotations—royalty, but a casual beach vibe. I was oblivious to the problems. I thought the purple motif would stand out against McDonald's, Burger King, and Wendy's, all of which used red, yellow, and orange in their color palettes. And my colors *did* stand out, but not in the way I wanted them to. I didn't realize their colors had been chosen after thousands of hours of research and marketing. There was a reason why the successful fast-food chains relied on bold, bright colors to draw in customers. They had done their homework, and they knew what would work.

But I wasn't interested in market research. I had been so successful in the past that I was confident my winning streak would continue. My success had blinded me. I knew what I liked and assumed others would like it as well. This type of overconfidence and reliance on intuition had been my strength in the past, but it would prove to be instrumental in my undoing.

The interior of WUV's included fuchsia and white plastic chairs, purple tile, and plastic greenery. The original exteriors were purple and white. The colors and materials were attractive to me, and everything looked clean and orderly. The interior of the stores really did look sensational, and, at the time, modern. It was just all wrong for a restaurant that specialized in burgers and fries.

Despite all my mistakes in marketing, I had done one thing exactly right: WUV's product was exceptionally strong. I had always believed it was best to do one thing exceptionally rather than do many things that were mediocre. When I came up with our menu, I limited it to hamburgers, fried chicken, salads, chili, French fries, onion rings, and biscuits. I insisted on the highest quality ingredients. While the preparation would take more time, and the costs would be higher, I believed it was a tradeoff I was willing to make. People would pay a little bit more for good food.

The biggest red flag that should have alarmed me was how much of my own money was on the line. I had invested millions of my own dollars to get WUV's off the ground. But I thought I had a fool-proof plan. I'd gone to the bank and gotten them to agree: if I ever needed it, they would match my investment dollar for dollar. We signed a contract and I felt confident that the *last* thing that could go wrong was that we'd run out of money. So I forged ahead.

Customers and food critics all agreed the quality of our food was fantastic. Our burgers were 100 percent lean ground beef without fillers or scraps. They were fresh—never frozen—and they were juicy and flavorful. We kept the skin on our fresh potatoes before we cut them into French fries. Our onion rings were made from whole onions, not bits and pieces. There was a full salad bar with toppings such as fresh vegetables and high-quality dressings, and I quickly added "WUV's Bites" to the menu—strips of chicken, fish, and steak. While they were labor intensive to make, they were delicious.

Food was cooked to order at WUV's, which reflected a growing fast-food trend in the mid 1970s. Burger King had begun their "Have it Your Way" campaign the same year. WUV's customizable menu fit right in. Our taglines were "Get Fresh at WUV's" and "A Fresh Idea in Fast Food." Customers loved it. Even today, there are websites and social media pages dedicated to the fond memories made with WUV's food. I believed then, and still believe now, that our menu boasted the finest quality fast food anywhere in the industry.

In addition to the menu, perhaps one of my greatest assets was my staff. Everyone—from the grill cook in the back to the cashier in the front—was properly trained. I had instituted employee incentives to keep them motivated and aggressive. Our focus would be on customer service with satisfaction. I wanted each customer to have a positive dining experience at WUV's.

With outstanding food and employees, I was bursting with confidence in late 1975 when I opened my first WUV's in Boca Raton, Florida. My return to the fast-food industry was an exciting time. I was surprised at how much I had missed it. I knew I had a lot of long hours ahead of me, but I had never shied away from hard work.

I should have known better. I began to lose control of the brand. I hired an attorney who had worked with the franchises at McDonald's. I told him I wanted to be set up just like McDonald's was. See, McDonald's isn't really a burger franchise—it's a real estate mogul. Instead of making money from its franchisees by charging high franchise fees, McDonald's simply becomes a landlord. They buy the properties, build the stores, and charge rent at a high mark-up. Then the corporation takes a percentage of each store's gross sales, lining their pockets with cash to invest in other properties to buy and turn for a profit. While there are almost 40,000 locations worldwide, only about 15 percent are owned *and* operated by McDonald's corporation. That's how I wanted to structure WUV's.

At first I did a lot of it myself. I washed my own potatoes. I made the hamburger patties by hand. I kept food fresh and the restaurant clean. Despite the fact that I had millions of dollars in the bank, I wouldn't have felt right if I hadn't rolled up my sleeves and gotten my hands dirty. I have always believed I can't ask people to do a job I was unwilling to do myself. I preferred to manage by example. I believed that with my attention to detail, I could turn WUV's into the next big thing. If it didn't become a success, it wouldn't be for lack of effort.

For a while, things went far better than I had anticipated. I had conservatively projected we'd do a weekly volume of around $3,000. But by the end of the first week, we had nearly doubled our expectations. The first WUV's had a drive-through window, an emerging concept at the time. As cars lined up to buy our food and customers crowded inside the restaurant, my confidence grew. WUV's was on its way to becoming a success, just like I knew it would. By the end of the first year, we were doing more than $13,000 in volume per week. People loved our fresh approach to fast food. Word of mouth was phenomenal. We were a hit.

So much of business success comes down to timing, and I had always had a natural instinct for choosing the right moment to make a move. I decided to strike while the iron was hot, expanding quickly to create some buzz. Within the first year, I opened 16 restaurants. I wasn't worried about handling such an all-consuming task. After all, I opened 16 McDonald's locations about two years before. Ideally, I should have kept the new locations close to home so I could monitor their operations, but my second restaurant was in Little Rock, Arkansas. All was going well. Then I started opening in tourist locations: Atlanta, Chattanooga, Tampa, and Orlando. I liked the idea of happy customers returning home, talking about the amazing restaurant they had visited.

And it totally worked. Within months, I began to get calls from people who were interested in opening WUV's franchises all over the country. My knack for creating hype hadn't failed me. I was confident I would eventually be able to compete with McDonald's and Burger King for fast-food dominance. Things were falling into place.

Upstart chains have different franchising challenges than existing chains do. McDonald's had a stronger, wider base. They had name recognition and greater financial stability. For a brand-new chain like WUV's, I had to be careful about who I picked to franchise our concept. I couldn't afford to make any mistakes.

And it turned out to come back to bite me. In my excitement about the rapid expansion, I neglected to properly vet the franchisees, leading to overwhelming logistical nightmares. My first franchisee was a businessman from Fort Smith, Arkansas, a small city on the Arkansas-Oklahoma border. It would be our first location west of the Mississippi, nearly 1,200 miles from our offices. I couldn't reach it easily—the nearest major airport was in Little Rock, 100 miles away. Because the location was so remote, I could only hope that he was doing things correctly.

With the help of my new attorney, I was certain we would get the franchising back under control. Although we made some mistakes, our concept and product were still a cut above the rest. And besides, every new company stumbles while starting out—not all of those falls are fatal. I continued to be optimistic about our future.

Within the next two years, we opened locations in California, New Jersey, and Michigan. I spent a lot of time flying to locations in a desperate attempt to maintain uniformity. I opened three offices—one in Fort Lauderdale, one in Chicago, and one in L.A. I visited each office every week. The offices helped with logistics, but they also cost a lot of money—funds that I shouldn't have been spending. I saw my finances hemorrhaging before my very eyes. Franchises would close, seemingly overnight, leaving me responsible for their expenses. I would find a new franchisee and repeat the same destructive pattern.

By the late 1970s, we were having some problems at the very foundation of WUV's. Some costs were spiraling out of control.

While we could minimize some of the charges, other expenses were unavoidable. WUV's was facing many of the same struggles that challenged all businesses of that time.

The market was not on my side. Jimmy Carter was the president, and the slumping economy was frequently driving restaurants out of business. Interest rates began to climb dramatically. They quickly went from 7 percent to 21 percent. Inflation skyrocketed. When we could get a bank loan, the interest would be astronomical. I was paying 33 percent interest on financing all my equipment. It seemed that everything was falling apart due to circumstances beyond my control.

Things went from bad to worse. On November 4, 1979, Iranian rebels took 52 Americans hostage at the U.S. Embassy. A week later, President Carter imposed an oil embargo on Iran, leading to an energy crisis. As fuel prices increased, so did the cost of our supplies. Our profits began to collapse. During our monthly meetings, we would learn that four franchises had opened but three had closed. We couldn't get the foothold we needed, and things were growing more and more economically unstable.

We weren't the only restaurant going through hard times. McDonald's growth slowed to a halt during the late 1970s. Burger King's profits dropped 8 percent. And Wendy's, the company where I could have been working, had put a moratorium on new restaurants. Things were tough all over.

Despite our mounting financial woes, I somehow managed to keep a positive outlook—a benefit of a lifetime of optimism. Although I was under a staggering amount of stress, I was able to focus on making WUV's a success. Still, I knew that many of my employees and partners were feeling the pressure of our economic problems. I hired a comptroller named Steven Starace. He moved from New Jersey in 1978 to work with me, and he bore the brunt of a lot of the money issues.

Despite the enormous weight on his shoulders, he remained loyal and dependable, working hard and giving the best advice he could give me. He was a young guy, just 24 years old, and he wanted to do a good job. One weekend, he wanted to return to New Jersey for a wedding. I told him to write himself a check for $600 so he could make the trip. I knew how tight money was, but he more than deserved it.

I learned many employees would stick with me through the hard times if I simply showed them some appreciation and loyalty. Employment is a two-way street. A good relationship between a boss and employee is mutually beneficial—a concept that employers often neglect to show their workers. My appreciation of Steve's contribution to WUV's wasn't disingenuous. It has always been completely sincere. Through his loyalty, he became more than an employee—he became a trusted advisor and friend. More than 35 years later, he still works for me. I trust him completely.

It felt like things were a precarious house of cards—things could collapse at any moment. In 1979, a potential franchisee backed out of WUV's and wanted his $15,000 deposit back. We were broke, but there was a glimmer of hope—another businessman was coming in to sign a franchise agreement and pay us $10,000. If everything worked out, we would be fine. But when the second franchisee came in to meet with us, he showed up without his check.

"There was a fire in my car," he claimed. "The firemen sprayed foam all over my checkbook." We started to hear farfetched excuses like that all the time. Clearly, everyone was dealing with financial problems in their own way.

As things continued to fall apart, there was a singular bright spot in the darkness. I had married again, and in the spring of 1978, I found out I was going to be a father for the fourth time. On December 24, just three days after the energy crisis further crippled our business, my third daughter was born. We named her Nicole Lauren Penrod. From the very beginning, Nikki was a happy, optimistic child with a wide smile and bubbly personality. She was pure sunshine. I was 39, but she made me feel much younger. I fell in love with her immediately. Even during the uncertain times of the late 1970s, I felt grounded and stable when I was around my new daughter—she added warmth to my life.

Even during the hardest of times, I was devoted to all four of my children. My three older children were now entering adolescence. Michele was 13, Tracey was 11, and Michael was 9. Their needs were completely different from those of Nicole, and I made every effort to be an important part of their lives. Even though WUV's took up an inordinate about of my time, I refused to be an absentee dad. Sometimes I would take the kids with me to the Bahamas, but at other times our time together was less spectacular—sitting at home, talking about life. Those were my favorite times.

I looked for fun and a break from the grind wherever I could find it—sometimes at the expense of my long-suffering friends. On a trip to the Bahamas, I flew my plane with my old friend Pete Bonitatibus sitting next to me. Suddenly, without warning, I took the plane into a barrel roll. As Pete shouted obscenities at me while we were upside down, I couldn't stop laughing. When we were upright, he yelled, "What the hell is wrong with you? Are you trying to kill me?" He hollered for a few minutes, but I could tell he was trying not to laugh. As he calmed down, he pointed out that I was not an experienced enough pilot to do a barrel roll, especially with him in the passenger seat. He was right, of course, but I still thought it was funny—and Pete still tells that story to this day.

But the moments of fun became few and far between. I began to think of ways to save WUV's, and my ideas became more and more desperate. One day, I came into the office with a plan. "Let's serve freshly baked chocolate chip cookies at WUV's"—not that a cookie was going to save the restaurant, but I figured they'd at least create some momentum. The idea made sense to me. The aroma of freshly baked cookies would entice customers. No one else was offering fresh cookies—it would help set us apart from the competition. Best of all, it would require a minimum investment of time and money.

It wasn't a terrible idea, but it was overly optimistic. The financial problems at WUV's were so severe that it would take more than a few cookies to save us. Our menu was clearly not the problem—people loved what we were selling. The problem was everything else about WUV's—the name, the colors, and the locations. Not to mention the abysmal economy. When we introduced the cookies, customers loved them. Despite adding another successful item to our menu, they made little difference in our bottom line—but the locations sure did smell wonderful!

There was a lot of irony in the failure of WUV's. In many ways, it was a victim of its own success and growth. Our business model had been built on fresh ingredients that took a great deal of preparation—it's what made our food stand out from other fast food. When volumes were low, this commitment to freshness was easy to maintain. As our restaurants grew busier, it became much more difficult and expensive. The preparations of fresh ingredients required us to hire workers who were above average in skill—and in compensation. I had developed a great concept, but it was labor-intensive.

I considered diluting our product, something I never would have contemplated in the early days of WUV's. Perhaps we could freeze some of our food? Maybe some things could be made in bulk? Or perhaps we could choose less expensive ingredients? The very ideas were awful to me—doing any of these things would feel like I was giving up on the very concept of fresh fast food. As I examined my options, I understood what had happened to McDonald's. As their volume skyrocketed, they began to freeze their burgers and fries, resulting in an inevitable drop in their quality. At the time, I had wondered why they would do such a thing. Why would you serve anything that wasn't the very best quality? Now the answer was clear: McDonald's had lowered their food standards to make more money. Although I understand what happened, it was out of the question for WUV's to do the same thing. I decided that no matter what happened, we would never scrimp on quality to survive.

We were blowing through money. I went back to the bank that had guaranteed me money in the event of a crisis just like this. But the banks weren't immune to Carter's interest rates either. They had declared bankruptcy, which allowed them to declare the contract we had signed as void. I reached out to my suppliers. "You'll get paid," I told them. "Just give me a little more time to turn things around."

As things grew bleaker in 1980, my advisors encouraged me to consider filing for bankruptcy. At first I wouldn't hear of it. To me, bankruptcy would mean failure. I was doggedly determined to succeed. Even in the worst of times, I clung to a positive outlook. Then my advisors showed me the books—there was seemingly no escape. Although the writing was clearly on the wall, I didn't want to quit. I continued to hang on, hoping that our fortunes would change. Things were so bad that I figured they could only get better.

In 1981, our fortunes did change—but not for the better. Franchises began closing at an alarming rate, and no new ones stepped in to take their place. I flew to Michigan for two restaurant launches. They were complete failures, and neither ever made a profit. There were no bright spots left in WUV's. Failure was inevitable. Sadly, reluctantly, I knew what I had to do. I called my lawyer and threw in the towel. It was by far the most difficult decision I ever had to make, but the game I was playing wasn't fun anymore. For the first time, because the government changed the rules on me, I was losing.

On December 22, 1981, the headline on the front page of the *Miami Herald* said it all: "Another Dynasty Dissolves." The article reported all the pertinent details—WUV's had filed for Chapter 11 bankruptcy. I was going to file for personal bankruptcy. We had released more of our staff. We were closing locations. And next to the story was my headshot.

Once the story hit the wires, other media called me for a comment. "We got ourselves in a hole, and we can't get out of it," I told the *New York Times*. The story reminded its readers that I had once predicted to have 500 WUV's locations by 1981. As it stood, we only had 70. We had lost $1 million in 1981 on revenues of $5 million. The bankruptcy filing was public—the numbers were available to anyone who wanted to know about our finances. Everyone knew that I had failed.

There was a lot of turmoil, and I was emotionally tapped out. I was devastated and embarrassed, but mostly I was exhausted. The previous five years had taken their toll on me. I felt beaten down.

I actually can't remember a single detail about the bankruptcy filing. It's all a blur. I had paid back as many of the little people as I could but defaulted on some of the larger debts. The bankruptcy trustee ordered my assets be taken away. They towed my cars. They took my wristwatch. They took everything except my home because in the state of Florida, they can't take your house. The only other thing they didn't take was my island, Scotland Cay, because it wasn't in my name. Even though I still owned it, I didn't even have a way to get there—they had also taken my boat and my plane.

On a personal level, I had learned some very expensive lessons. I could have saved myself a lot of money if I had been more careful with the distribution of my personal wealth. I had neglected to protect my assets properly. If I had invested my money in trust accounts and with family members, I would have been able to access some of my funds for this *very* rainy day. I should have had offshore accounts to protect myself. It was a mistake I would never make again.

I had gotten into too much debt—I drowned in it. There is a lot of value in doing business with other people's money—it can help grow a business. But after WUV's failure, I decided never to get in that type of debt again. Thirty years later, all my businesses are 100 percent mine. I don't go into debt. It adds a level of stability and security to everything I do.

Bankruptcy was my worst nightmare come true. So much of my adult life had been wrapped up in my success. Now I had failed. Even the word "bankrupt" sounded like "failure" to me. It was the darkest time of my professional career. But I will tell you one bit of relief I had: the day after I filed, my phone was silent—not a single debt collector hounding me. It was wonderful.

My brother Bob was doing very well. He owned a profitable club in Atlanta called Penrod's People Parlor. It packed in crowds every weekend. I had helped him out several times in the past—it was now time for him to return the favor. He sent me an old Camaro with a broken seat that was held up by a baseball bat. I used that vehicle to get around for months. It was a taste of humility, but honestly, I didn't mind. I was grateful for my health, for my children, and for the opportunity to try again.

Despite my disappointment, I knew I had learned a lot of valuable lessons that would follow me for the rest of my life. For every business venture I've undertaken since WUV's, I've developed a clear concept of my objectives and goals. I do my research before making big decisions.

I also learned to be careful who I go into business with. Many of my franchisees had oversold their qualifications. They had told me they had more money and abilities than they actually had. I learned the importance of always looking at the facts as I am qualifying potential partners. I know I wouldn't be as successful as I am today if I hadn't walked through the bankruptcy.

Shortly after I lost everything, I walked along a bridge in Fort Lauderdale. When I was halfway across it, I looked down at the water. All I had to do was climb over a flimsy railing to escape the uphill climb ahead. Lots of guys jump to their deaths over a lot less than what I'd been through. But that wasn't me. I'm not an easy-way-out kind of guy.

Besides, it didn't make sense for me to end it all over financial problems. I had grown to learn that there's more to life than money. *And* that there's always more money to be made—if you're willing to keep trying.

I continued over the bridge and sat down on the beach, staring at the skyline. In the distance, I saw a hotel—the Yankee Trader. I had heard of the place. The owner, Bob Gill, had just opened a newer, second tower. I had heard at a party the year prior that he was trying to open a club in the older, first tower. I wondered how that club was doing. The possibilities started filtering through my mind, building in both excitement and urgency. I needed to get home to my yellow legal pad to write down my ideas.

I had four children who I needed to take care of. I wasn't ready to give up just yet.

THE KING OF SPRING BREAK

"I try not to make the same mistakes over and over again. Every failure and every success is a lesson. It takes some thought and some reflection to learn the lessons life puts in front of you. As I rebuilt my career from the ashes of WUV's, I tried to incorporate many of the things I had learned. I knew I would be a success again; I just needed to find a new opportunity. Maybe it was time to move away from the fast-food industry. I was open to anything."

—JACK

With the devastating failure of WUV's, I found myself at an unfamiliar crossroads in my career. For the first time in several years, I didn't have any particular agenda. Six years earlier, I had been rich enough that I never had to work again. Now I was relatively young—only 42—but I was flat broke with four kids to raise. I always had my eyes open, looking for the next opportunity. But unlike the last time, where I built a business opportunity on some Hawaiian prints and a tag on a stuffed animal, I would make careful and deliberate choices. I had tasted failure, and I didn't like it. I was *not* going to repeat the same mistakes.

In a strange way, there were some similarities to where I had been six years earlier. Again, I found myself in a position where I was willing to take risks—measured risks.

There was some liberation in having nothing to lose, and I was willing to go in a brand-new direction. On some level, I had the same excitement as before—that I was on the cusp of brand-new opportunities. All I needed to do was keep an open mind and heart as I looked for my next big thing.

As it turned out, I had made some fortunate choices long before I had declared bankruptcy, and those choices laid the groundwork for my future success. The previous year, I had gone to a Fort Lauderdale nightclub for a cocktail party. It was a surprising decision for me—I wasn't much of a drinker, and I don't usually care for small talk. But for some reason, I had decided to go.

It turned out to be a highly beneficial networking opportunity. That was the party where I learned about the underperforming nightclub. I met a contact there who chatted with me for a long time about the challenges the club was experiencing. After that night on the bridge, I decided to take a trip to the club to see how it was faring.

My entire background was in the fast-food industry. In 1981, I knew very little about nightclubs. During my years at McDonald's and WUV's, however, I had learned a lot about marketing and promotions. I was an expert at creating a buzz. While the club industry was different from anything I had done before, I knew that many of my skills would carry over to this new opportunity—if I could get my foot in the door. My goal would be to draw in customers and create an experience that would bring them back again and again. Generally speaking, customers' needs are the same whether you're selling them hamburgers or Champagne.

The hotel was called the Yankee Trader, a pleasant beachfront property on A1A that would eventually become a Sheraton. It was in a great location. I drove over to the hotel in my old Camaro. Arriving unannounced, I walked through the Showplace, a club area on the bottom two floors. The owners had spent a fortune renovating it. It was a well-planned, modern space, made up of several distinct rooms. Downstairs, there was a large room decorated like a saloon, separated from a disco by two glass doors. Upstairs was a beautiful ballroom with high ceilings and luxurious décor. It was a tasteful, inviting location.

But I quickly realized that an attractive space did not necessarily ensure crowds of customers. I strolled into the club during evening hours—when business should be at its peak—but there wasn't a single customer in the entire place. The attractive bartenders stood idly by, making small talk with each other. Some of them were literally sitting on the bar. No one had anything to do.

Bored, unenthusiastic employees can be fatal to a club—or to any business, for that matter. Their disinterest can be contagious. People are drawn to other people who seem to be having a good time. The bartenders at the Showplace were clearly not enjoying themselves. Despite the inviting décor and the convenient location, the entire vibe of the club was boring. The club would need an infusion of energy if it were going to survive. If I could find a way to fill up half the club with an excited, energetic crowd, the other half would fill itself.

A large, unused space is costly to a hotel, and it was obvious that Yankee Trader would have been financially better off if the Showplace closed. Not only was it failing to earn revenue, but it was losing money every month. With the employees and upkeep, the overhead was astronomical. Quite simply, the club was a bad investment. I was on familiar ground. I had spent the previous 20 years trying to minimize overhead. I had learned several tricks to make sure I wouldn't fall into the same trap.

I asked around to find out who was running the place. Bob Gill still owned it, so I reached out to him. Sure enough, he asked me to take a look at the hotel club to see whether I could help turn its fortunes around. Without anything else on the horizon, I decided to give it a shot.

I did some market research. Despite all its problems, the Showplace should have been doing brisk business. It was in a prime location. I left the club and walked along the street. Several nightclubs dotted A1A, all with thriving nightlife. Happy, attractive people drank, danced, and partied just a few dozen feet from this gorgeous venue. The sidewalks were flooded with foot traffic. Cars drove along the strip all night long, full of young adults who were looking for a good time. The entire scene of Fort Lauderdale was electrifying—except for the Showplace. There was no reason why it should have been empty—they were clearly doing something very wrong.

I was ready to work with the Showplace, but it had to be on my terms. I met with Mr. Gill and gave him my assessment: the club was worth saving, but it would take a lot of hard work to turn things around. We chatted about the updated decor and the strength of the location. I also pointed out the liabilities and possibilities. Mr. Gill was all ears.

"So," he finally asked, "what would you do to make money where I couldn't?"

"It's magic," I replied with a smile. "I know what to do, but it will take hard work and imagination." He didn't seem immediately convinced. "I'll do with it what I did to McDonald's," I continued. "I will develop my own concept."

To fortify my chances of getting the job, I reached out to my brother Bob. After I sold my McDonald's stores, I'd given him a million dollars. He took the money, went to Atlanta, and opened a bunch of bars called Penrod's. "Bob," I told him, "send me one of your menus. I need to prove I can run this bar."

When I met with Mr. Gill again, I showed him what my brother had sent me. "Yeah, " I told him, "this is a family business." Which was, at least technically, the truth.

I wanted the gig. The more I thought about it, the more I knew I could handle the task if given the chance. I also knew that Bob Gill would probably have to give me a chance to turn things around. After all, he had nothing to lose.

After our meeting, I went home and wrote out a three-page contract on a yellow legal pad—just like I had with McDonald's. I offered to take over the property and turn it into a success. But, according to the contract, I would not spend my own money on the venture. I was not going to pay rent, utilities, insurance, or taxes on a location that was already underperforming. Instead, I offered to pay them 50 percent of my bottom line or $100,000 a year—whichever was higher. It would still be a risk for me—I was investing my time and effort on a venture that could easily fail. But I was not going to go bankrupt again, and I refused to go into debt to turn this club around. I was confident but playing it safe—playing it smart. On the third sheet of paper, I mapped out my expected profits for the first few years.

My predictions turned out to be conservative, but I showed him some ways the Showplace would become profitable. Mr. Gill and I sat and negotiated the terms.

"I need you to produce an income of at least $100,000 during one of the first five years," he said.

I knew he was being lenient, or maybe he'd never considered that the bar could do that well. Either way, my self-belief and experience had not only gotten me in the door but had given me a two-story club and another opportunity for adventure.

I now had several chances to make the Showplace into a success—and I was doing it without paying rent and overhead. In effect, it would be as if I had owned the property forever. I just needed to leverage it successfully.

Perhaps it was a risky move for the Showplace to hire a hamburger man to turn their nightclub around, but it was happening at the right time for both of us. Neither of us had anything to lose and everything to gain. They were bleeding money with no turnaround in sight. I had been embarrassed on a national level and was searching for a new opportunity. We were both outside our comfort zones.

If there was one thing I had learned—and continue to learn—throughout my career, it's that comfort zones are overrated. Many times, comfort can equal stagnation. I have only experienced true growth when I pushed myself past the boundaries of what I thought was safe and secure. My rewards have always been borne out of calculated risk. I have tried to be smart about my decisions, but I have never avoided some degree of uncertainty. Had I never taken risks, I would still be working poolside at the Greenbrier, and my destiny would have been unfulfilled.

But I wanted the risks to be calculated risks. I didn't want to stupidly proceed with something that had no chance of working. After crunching the numbers, I decided the Showplace would be an acceptable risk for me. I signed a five-year contract. I incorporated Penrod's Restaurant, Inc. Then it was time to roll up my sleeves and get to work. The Showplace would now be called Penrod's on the Beach. I was in the nightclub business.

Before the ink on the contract was dry, I began to brainstorm ways to turn things around for the club. Marketing strategy had always been my forte, and I knew exactly what demographic I needed to target. As I did with McDonald's, I knew that if I could get attractive girls to show up, the young men would follow. I had to figure out a way to make Penrod's on the Beach a hotspot for the younger crowd. If I could do that, we'd make a fortune.

Shortly after starting Penrod's, I decided to open a second location nearby. I found Elbo Room, a 50-year-old bar located on the corner of A1A and Las Olas Boulevard on Fort Lauderdale Beach. It had just a touch of old Hollywood glamour. The 1960s movie *Where the Boys Are* had filmed at the bar. But time had not been kind to Elbo Room, and it was going through bankruptcy. I knew they were desperate for someone who could run the business competently, and I was ready to go for it.

I signed a different deal with the Elbo Room than I had with the Showplace. The landlord had been running the building for more than 40 years, and it was time for him to retire—except for one thing. He had leased the property for 100 years at $1,200 a year. He thought it was too high, so he got them to lower it to $1,000 a year for 100 years. With 60 years remaining on the lease, the landlord wanted to sublease the property. The terms of the lease would be high. I paid him $100,000 per year, but I knew what the volume could be.

If I could bring in customers to Elbo Room, I would make a lot of money. On October 16, 1981, I incorporated Penrod's Elbo Room, Inc. Excited at the prospect of having two locations, I signed a five-year lease with ten additional five-year options. More than 30 years later, I still own Elbo Room. My three oldest kids run it, and they're making a fortune. It has been one of my most profitable ventures per square foot of space.

In the early 1980s, "spring break" was becoming part of the American lexicon, and I wanted to take it to the next level. I needed to turn Fort Lauderdale into the prime destination for spring break. If my locations could make enough revenue during those critical weeks, we could muddle through the slower months of the year. My goal wasn't necessarily to turn Fort Lauderdale into an iconic spring break location; I simply wanted to bring potential customers to town. Creating hype is worthless if it doesn't translate into increased sales and volume. Everything I did was intended to help my businesses become more profitable.

I needed to get the city to rally around the idea of bringing busloads of college students to town. I found an ally in Virginia Shuman Young, the first female mayor of Fort Lauderdale. Ambitious, intelligent, and open-minded, Mayor Young wanted to leave her mark on the city. She thought spring break would be just the way to do it. She saw college students as future professionals.

"These kids will someday be doctors and lawyers," she reasoned. "Maybe they'll fall in love with the area and become taxpaying citizens."

An expanded spring break would be a boon for hotels, merchandise, restaurants, and nightclubs. We shared the same vision. With her on board, I promised to work on bringing more students to town. It seemed like a no-brainer to me.

With a plan in place, I threw myself into marketing Fort Lauderdale to college students. I took two busses of beautiful people on a 129-city college campus tour. We'd hand out pamphlets to students with hotel names and event itineraries all plastered with our slogan, "Come on down to Florida!" This wasn't a money-making endeavor—I was trying to raise awareness of Fort Lauderdale. We advertised in newspapers and on college radio stations. We got permission to set up tables on campuses that we placed attractive young people behind to personally recruit potential spring-breakers. We were everywhere.

Students were receptive to the idea of Fort Lauderdale—it was easy to market to them. We told them the weather would be great and the beaches superb. The community would welcome them with open arms. In colleges across the country, students began making their plans to spend their spring break in our city.

Knowing we were going to get an influx of young guests, I had to make sure there were enough activities for them at my clubs. During the day, I organized some fun events on the beach. At night, I organized club events to keep them coming back. It wasn't rocket science. I held bikini contests and toga parties. We had hot-dog eating contests. There were punk rock concerts and special events, all planned to show the students a good time. I knew they would return to college and talk about the rowdy times they had in Fort Lauderdale. With the right mix of promotion and activities, our numbers would climb exponentially.

One of the best ideas I had for spring break in Fort Lauderdale was an event called "Feed Your Face." In the lull of the afternoon, students could pay ten bucks for unlimited pasta and breadsticks. I also threw in a free beer mug, a T-shirt, and a pair of sunglasses—which was a hell of a bargain.

Of course, to make this event profitable, I had to shop my promotional merchandise, keeping costs low. I'd get the sunglasses for a quarter each, the shirts for 80 cents. For the unlimited beer, you had to go to the one bar I kept open. You were lucky to get two beers at any given time because it was so busy.

Feed Your Face turned out to be one of the most well-attended spring break events I held because it met a critical need—feeding broke and hungover kids who had time to kill and a penchant to socialize all hours of the day and night.

Now, the kids came down to spring break with, let's say, 50 dollars in their pockets. It was my goal to unload them of every cent—not to swindle them out it, but to exchange the experience of their lives for their money.

I did have my moral limits. I never did wet T-shirt contests with my college events. The bikini contests were enough of a draw. People would arrive early for a front-row seat. All the pretty girls from miles around came to compete because the prize was $1,000 cash. I would make some of the city officials judges in order to keep in good with the city.

I had confidence in our plans and events, but even I could not have predicted how well our marketing would work. The numbers surprised me. In 1980, Fort Lauderdale had 50,000 spring-breakers. The next year, in February and March 1981, there were 130,000 visitors. Then it happened: In the winter of 1983, the movie *Spring Break* was a box-office smash, depicting Fort Lauderdale as a binge of beer, parties, and wet T-shirts.

It wasn't too far off.

That same year, a *Mad Magazine* cartoonist—commissioned by the Tourist Department Council—drew a now-famous poster showing hordes of scantily clad sorority girls lounging on the beach. More than 200,000 college students showed up for spring break that year. Everybody was happy. The students were generally well-behaved. They pumped a lot of money into the economy. And then they went home and told all their friends about the great time they had had in Fort Lauderdale. Everything I had planned with Mayor Young was coming to fruition.

But it wasn't done growing yet. By 1984, there were 300,000 spring-breakers, all trying to top the parties from the year before. Businesses in the area were making money—and a lot of it. Hotels were packed to capacity, charging higher rates than usual. Restaurants had lines around the block. Merchandise flew off the shelves. Penrod's had never been more successful. During the first five years, I netted $4 million for Bob Gill. We were both very happy with the results.

I was smarter with my money this time. I invested in trusts for my children, ensuring they'd be able to go to college if they chose to, or to have the freedom to learn a trade if that's what they wanted to do. I sent most of the rest of my money offshore. No, I wouldn't make the same mistakes again.

In fact, I was on my way toward a pinnacle so high, even I could not predict the adventures still to come.

EXPANSION

"In all my companies, I have learned the importance of hiring key people—and the necessity of listening to them. Sometimes the right employees will come up with ideas that I would never have dreamed of. While I made the final decisions at all my clubs, I had learned it was wise to get multiple opinions before I decided to proceed."

—JACK

I had a marketing office at one of the clubs. It was a small room—nothing fancy—and I kept an open-door policy. I would listen to everyone's suggestions. Some of the ideas were great; others were terrible. But it was important to me to seriously consider any viable suggestion to market our clubs.

Little by little, I bought up hotels and clubs all over Fort Lauderdale. Before it was all said and done, I owned every bar except two. See, when I brought all these people into town, there was no way I could handle them all between the Showroom and Elbo Room—there were just too many people. If I wanted a cut of the profits I was bringing in, I needed to have my name on more deeds.

My design instincts had also locked in. At the Showroom, I re-modeled the office areas to entertain the increasing number of students. I had a room called "The Dungeon." I had a concert room for live bands. In another room, I held bikini contests. The money was coming in faster than we could track it.

By the mid 1980s—just a few years after my bankruptcy—I was riding high once again. During the first seven months of 1985, my Fort Lauderdale locations had grossed more than $3.5 million. The newspapers began writing stories about me, calling me a "Spring Break Magnate." I had become the go-to guy for marketing the city.

But Fort Lauderdale was changing. Virginia Young was no longer mayor. She had been replaced by Robert Dressler, who wasn't as enthusiastic about the idea of spring break. Under Mayor Dressler, Fort Lauderdale merely tolerated the events—they certainly did nothing more to encourage it. Much of the marketing stopped. I realized that spring break had been the remedy Fort Lauderdale had desperately needed before, but it was time to shift gears and give Fort Lauderdale what it needed *now*.

Fortunately, I had anticipated this development. Elbo Room's five-year lease was up, and I spoke with the landlord. We came up with a similar deal to what I had with the Yankee Trader, which had since become a Sheraton. We entered a zero-based lease where I would pay no rent. Instead, I agreed to pay him 50 percent of the income. Although he was worried about the lack of volume, he didn't want to run the bar himself. As spring break waned and profits dropped, I reinvented Elbo Room into a more sophisticated beach bar. The crowds of tourists got slightly older—and slightly wealthier. They spent a lot of money at Elbo Room, and profits returned to where they had been during the spring-break heyday.

Around this time, I went to a boat show and saw a fishing boat that looked really nice. I found the sales guy and pointed: "I'll take that boat."

The sales guy had a look on his face like, *Huh?*

So I bought the boat, and I heard about this huge fishing expedition they were having the next day. There were about ten boats going, and I said, "Sign me up."

I invited my brother-in-law, and we headed out with the other boats. The first night we were out, we came up on this huge storm—I mean, it was big. I don't know why the leader of the group didn't know about it, but weather equipment wasn't that good back then. The waves were monstrous—some at least 25 feet high.

The leader who owned the boat company said, "Let's go to shore."

We were right off of the southern tip of Cuba. We went into the shore, and all of a sudden, Jeeps came up on the ridge and jets started flying overhead. This voice came over a megaphone and said, "We demand that you leave immediately."

Back onto our boats we went. We got back out to sea, but nobody had prepared for that kind of storm—including me. I was the first to run out of fuel. Somehow we managed to tie our boats together. Someone was able to give me fuel, but I was taking on a whole lot of water.

Then, out of nowhere, I hit a wave—hard. My seat broke, the bar broke, and I fell to the cockpit below on my back. I got up slowly and crawled to the top of the boat so I could drive the thing.

I looked at my brother-in-law. "If someone would just come in a helicopter and get us," I yelled, "they can keep this f-ing boat!"

All I wanted was to be off that boat. By that point, I was seasick. We were in the fifteenth hour of the storm, and we probably had 15 more to go. There was nothing left to do but to endure, to try to stay alive and keep going until the storm quieted down.

Luckily, the boat was made out of metal; it was an all-aluminum boat. It could take a lot more than I could. We finally made it to our destination, but we were shaky at best.

I think it goes without saying, but I'll state the obvious—we may not have caught any fish on the expedition, but we certainly walked away with a whale of a story.

As I became entrenched in the Fort Lauderdale scene, I met hundreds of businessmen and colorful characters, but perhaps none of them were as colorful as Bernie Little. He was larger than life and frequently written up in the society pages of South Florida newspapers. He drove a Rolls Royce around town and wore a lot of jewelry.

Underneath the flashy exterior, Bernie was an astute businessman. He owned several businesses throughout the state and had made a big splash in powerboat racing. I met him during one of my promotional events, Penrod's Offshore Powerboat Racing. We hit it off quickly.

Bernie loved a faded Miami hotspot called the Jockey Club, perhaps because it was there that he parked his 110-foot yacht. The club's fortunes were fading; it was an underperforming, unexciting place. They asked me to turn things around.

With the expansion and diversity of my Penrod's brand, I needed new staff. As I had always done, I chose the best people possible. In 1984, a young woman named Lucia Hausman came into our office through a temporary placement agency. She was brilliant—far beyond the talents of the secretarial position she had been hired for. She was exactly what I needed: organized, competent, and willing to learn. Only, when I offered to make her job permanent at the Jockey Club, she turned me down.

A native of Nicaragua, Lucia had come to the United States in 1979 in the midst of a socialist revolution to topple the dictatorship regime of her home country. Having been raised in Catholic school by well-to-do parents, Lucia settled in Miami and went to work for the consulates of South Korea and Venezuela. After spending five years working in the diplomatic field, Lucia decided to stay and pursue a career in event planning. While she built up her business, she'd applied at a temp agency.

"I cannot work for you full time, Mr. Penrod," she explained. "I want to be a wedding planner."

Not one to be deterred, I pushed. "How much do you think you can make as a wedding planner?" I asked her.

"Oh, I could do pretty well," she said. "I'd say around $50,000 a year."

"Done," I said. "I'll pay you $50,000 a year. Welcome to the team."

The fact that Lucia was beautiful had nothing to do with my decision to hire her. She has one of the sharpest minds I've come across in my career—and I still believe that. Besides, she was married, and I had married again as well. Our relationship would be strictly professional.

I was in my element. I brought in live shows. I had Miami Dolphin football players come to the club for autograph signings. Although the numbers started improving dramatically, not everyone was thrilled. The Jockey Club was a resident club, meaning that many of the nearby residents were automatically members. They were somewhat older, and they were disappointed that their nice, quiet club had become such a hotspot.

Despite some of the residents' objections, the Jockey Club owners were pleased with its reversal of fortune. After a year and a half, the management asked me to sign on as the general partner of the club. I considered the opportunity but ultimately decided to take my career in another direction. Disappointed, the acting general partner, Walter Troutman, decided to replace me. I moved on with no regrets.

Every opportunity leads to networking possibilities, and the Jockey Club had been no different. I met a man who owned a handful of underperforming hotels, including two Holiday Inns and a Sheraton. He asked me to fly to his home base of Philadelphia and look at them. After a quick trip to Pennsylvania, he and I signed a management agreement. I took over four of his hotels.

The hotels did well with business travel. Executives would stay for several weekdays at a time. During the weekends, however, the hotels were nearly vacant. The turnaround seemed quite simple: I added nightclubs that would create weekend business and offered reduced rates on Friday and Saturday nights.

But the hotels' biggest problem was their overhead. I began to assess where we were losing money. We had more than 20 automobiles, 3 trucks, and 2 warehouses filled with items we didn't need. Perhaps our biggest unnecessary expenditure was personnel. We had a complicated hierarchy of employees that often held redundant jobs. It was time to clean house.

As I cut expenses and increased revenues, the results were drastic. When I started, we were operating at a $1.8 million loss. Eighteen months later, we had an annual profit of more than $1 million. I didn't realize the owner was involved in some shady business deals, and I eventually decided it was time to move on—but I was proud of my track record. Besides, I was still busy figuring out spring break in Florida.

When spring break in Fort Lauderdale was still in full swing, Ron Kent, president of the Visitors and Convention Bureau from Miami Beach, came up to see if I would breathe some life into their community—they wanted me to bring spring break to their city. The age of the average citizen in Miami Beach at that time was 72. And, to be frank, 72-year-olds aren't known for their excessive spending habits. The city needed a revitalization—a return to their "American Riviera" days of the '50s.

To compound Miami Beach's aging demographic, it had only been a few years since Fidel Castro announced that all Cubans wishing to emigrate to the United States were free to board boats at the port of Mariel west of Havana—a move that would later come to be known as the Mariel boatlift. This would mark the arrival of the first of 125,000 Cuban refugees landing in South Florida. Because Castro had also opened the jails of Cuba, many of these newly minted Miamians were also convicted Cuban criminals.

They invited me to come down and take a look at their city to tell them if I thought I could do for them what I had done for Fort Lauderdale. I brought my new employee Lucia with me. She had a keen eye and was fluent in both English and Spanish—a language spoken by many of the residents in Miami.

We drove down the streets, and the sights were abysmal. There were droves of homeless people and thug-looking groups huddled on street corners. We even saw crack deals in progress and more than one person who had overdosed on drugs lying right on Ocean Drive. I learned that Social Security checks were regularly being stolen from mail boxes, the crime rate was up, and the reputation was down. Short of divine intervention, I didn't think there was anything I could do to save Miami Beach—it was nothing more than a slum. But more than my personal feelings about the endeavor, I refused to put my staff at risk in a city that dangerous.

I called Ron Kent. "Thanks," I said, "but no thanks."

The following year, Ron called again. This time he had a couple of Miami Beach commissioners on the line with him, including a man named Bruce Singer. "Tell us what it'll take to get you down here," they said. "Name your terms."

I was making big money at the Penrod's in Fort Lauderdale, and I had been spending a lot of time visiting Europe. I loved their beach clubs. I would talk to the owners, who were usually third- and fourth-generation owners. And these clubs kept enduring, just kept going on and on, because when you want a good time *or* you're having a hard time, you want to go to the beach. You want to go someplace where you feel like you're on holiday.

I decided I would open a beach club. I told the city of Miami, "If you give me everything I ask for, I'll make your city vibrant and wealthy."

They said, "Give us your wish list."

"Now, to be clear," I asked the commissioners, "what is the exact goal here?"

"I want you to lower the average age."

I knew I could do it. They gave me three miles of beachfront property where I put 2,000 lounge chairs. I wanted it to have an international feel. The city delegation didn't bat an eye at any of my demands. I was doing another deal at the time, so I sent Lucia down to handle my wishlist.

"This is what Mr. Penrod requires," she said, laying out my list of demands.

She did well because they acquiesced to every one of my requests. Lucia signed the lease on my behalf, and Penrod's Miami Beach was born.

At the time, Miami had a strange reputation across America. Two of the hottest shows on television were *Miami Vice* and *The Golden Girls*. At the theaters, audiences lined up to see Al Pacino in *Scarface*. Pop culture presented a skewed view of Miami Beach, and the American public's preconceived notions of Miami were often far different from reality. While it may have been glamorous on television in the eighties, the truth was much less attractive. Miami was a failing area with a lot of crime—but also a lot of potential. I knew I could make a difference.

Before I went there, there wasn't a single customer on the beach. The older people who owned the beachfront properties wouldn't go there because they were scared of the criminals and the drug and gang activity in the area. And it was a red zone—meaning, you couldn't borrow a penny there. I really was Miami Beach's only hope.

My first order of business was to make sure the elderly residents liked and trusted us. This wasn't a manipulative tactic—I didn't want to run them out. I wanted to bring a youthful energy to their town that wasn't exclusive or terribly intrusive. I believed then—and I do now—that spring break can be great for a community. So I threw a few dances for the senior citizens at the community center. I remember *USA Today* ran an ad about our work in Miami Beach with a grandpa and a group of young people, indicating that it was okay to be in the same space.

My strategy was simple—bring spring break to Miami for a limited time only to build up the area and improve the city's financial status and reputation. Why? Because college students are the only customers that don't really care about where they lay their heads, as long as there's beer and their friends are there.

In April 1985, I stood in front of the Miami Beach City Commission and outlined my plans to bring spring break to them. First and foremost, I wanted control of the beach. At the time, it was covered in needles and garbage and needed to be completely cleaned and re-built. I had plans to open three pink, portable concession stands on the beach of the art deco district. I wanted to build six permanent stands to offer parasailing, jet skiing, scuba gear, and roller skate rentals. And the biggest thing: I was building a large restaurant on One Ocean Drive that would seat 250 guests. At the time, the construction would cost $4 million. I was helping revitalize a blighted area. We were going to bring revenue to an area that desperately needed it. Most people were open to my vision.

But there was some opposition. Some of the elderly residents were still not convinced that spring break was a good idea. They were concerned that it could be dangerous or unpleasant. I spent a lot of time with them, convincing them it was okay to have some fun and that spring break would be a good thing for them and their community.

I wasn't trying to sell the old folks a bill of goods. I was trying to make money, but not at the expense of other people. I wanted everyone to be happy.

Instead of doing a bus tour this time, we jumped in a plane with Commissioner Bruce Singer and a representative from the *Miami Herald* who followed every step we made in the city. With the grant given to us from the city, we shipped sand and palm trees from Miami Beach all the way up to the Boston area to throw a promotional spring-break party at a club we'd negotiated terms with.

It was January 1986 in Boston, freezing cold with a foot of snow on the ground. There we were, with beach balls, girls in bikinis, lounge chairs, sand, and palm trees. The line to get inside our party went around the building. Kids were shivering and shaking but willing to wait out the below-30-degree weather to party "on the beach" with us.

It was extremely successful—both the event and the media attention it garnered. We still visited other college campuses, working to change the narrative of Miami Beach from the place your grandparents retire to and into the up-and-coming spring-break destination they couldn't miss. The buzz was already a roar.

The students showed up in droves. In addition, I wanted to attract international customers this time. So I dreamed a little bigger. One by one I told them, "If you're ever in South Beach, it's the hottest spot in the world right now." Then the Delanos opened their hotel, and all of a sudden, beach clubs and fancy hotels started popping up all along the Miami Beach coastline.

Working with the press can be a double-edged sword. While there is no way to completely control it, the media can be a valuable tool in marketing. Advertising can be very expensive, but news coverage—for the right reasons—is free and can be a huge boost to your business. Generally the press has always been fair to me, although there were times when they had their own agendas. By the time I expanded into Miami, I knew the value of creating events that would end up on the evening news. I sought to create these moments intentionally, knowing the attention would be good for everyone.

During our first year of spring break on Miami Beach, I went to Budweiser and had them sponsor one of our best attractions, a snow mountain right on the sand. I had a huge machine shaving tons of ice all night long, creating a two-story-tall frozen mountain. I hired an Olympian who had won the silver medal in downhill skiing in 1984. She would ski down the ice hill in front of crowds of cheering college students. The media picked up on the story and broadcast it around the world.

In fact, I talked MTV into coming out, and they filmed a spot where the skier slowly emerged from the ocean. First, you just see her snorkel, then you see her mask, and then she's coming out of the water, little by little, all with cool music playing. Then you see the skier walking on the sand and being the first one to ski down that slope. It was iconic—better than any advertising campaign I could imagine.

We didn't stop there.

We did toga parties. We held a mounted police invitational where we called all the mounted police from Florida and held competitions on the sand. Everything we were doing was in an effort to spread the word—not that a company had just come and tossed a few lounge chairs in Miami beach, but that Miami Beach was a unique destination for a younger crowd.

Spring break in Miami Beach started off slowly, and some hotels had expected to have Fort Lauderdale-like numbers in the first year. People started to grow impatient. Although many of them had expected more than 100,000 visitors to show up during the inaugural season, only a few thousand came. When the numbers fell short of their expectations, they began to worry I was mismanaging the promotions. Two years earlier, I had been dealing with angry crowds because I brought too many people to town; now I was dealing with impatient businessmen who said I wasn't bringing enough.

So we did spring break in Miami Beach in '86, '87, and in 1988. We used those three years to introduce people to the area in a safe way. By the time we were able to open our One Ocean Drive location, Miami Beach had become a very, very well-known area.

But that didn't stop me from marketing the heck out of it. I spent close to a million dollars advertising and promoting the grand opening of Penrod's Miami Beach. For six months before the club opened, our team met weekly to meticulously plan the week-long events and schedule.

We had a two-story building. On the bottom floor was the beach club, and upstairs there was a wonderful steakhouse. The opening happened to coincide with the 1990 Super Bowl between the Cincinnati Bengals and the San Francisco 49ers. We worked closely with the Miami Super Bowl committee to host one of their official welcome parties on a Friday before game day—it was amazing.

We had celebrity athletes like Joe Montana and Jerry Rice in attendance to watch the big game. And we gave them quite a show. We built bleachers and a huge, 30-foot television screen on the beach to broadcast the Super Bowl. There were games, events, and contests.

It was the biggest Super Bowl party I'd ever seen. But that was the goal—to be the biggest and the best. Though we'd had a soft opening the previous November, our January grand opening blew the lid off of everyone's expectations.

Everyone's but mine, that is. I knew we could pull it off all along.

When I first went down to Miami Beach, I tried to invite my friends with me as investors. I'd drive them around and show them the city, trying to help them see the city's potential. But back then, in the mid 1980s, no one was willing to roll the dice with me. After Penrod's Miami Beach opened, things started to change. The "big-time" New York investors swooped in and started snatching up real estate. Property values started rising. I joke that we did the dirty work in Miami for them. But in reality, that's not much of a joke!

Take, for example, our permanent concession stand on 10th Street in Lummus Park. It was broken into constantly in those early years, thieves stealing anything and everything they could get their hands on. One of our managers was even stabbed in the leg there. We had our work cut out for us when it came to cleaning up Miami Beach, but our team did it.

Though our name isn't mentioned in the history books as an important part of the renaissance of Miami Beach, I can tell you honestly that no one wanted to *touch* Miami Beach until we did. I put my money where nobody else wanted to. No one had faith in Miami Beach like I did.

Miami Beach was a buzz. However, with the influx of cash and crowds came traffic and trash. I wanted to be a good tenant in the city of Miami, so we hired a crew to walk the beach and roadways to pick up trash. They wore shirts that said "Penrod's Cleaning Crew" on them. But the city was starting to feel strained. The city manager, Rob Parkins, asked me to cut back on advertising to alleviate the explosion of visitors to the area.

We wanted to be good neighbors to the residents, so we did. Sometimes in business you have to make the difficult decision to lose money in order to do the right thing—in order to protect an important relationship and investment. But once you stop marketing, it's hard to maintain the same energy as an all-out campaign. When you're asked to pause, momentum is impossible to manufacture. Our bottom line was greatly affected, but it was the right decision for Miami Beach, which made it the right decision for us.

Elections were held, new leadership was put in charge, and the goals for Miami Beach shifted. We still had our beach club there, but business slowed immensely. There was plenty going on behind the scenes that needed my attention.

Lucia eventually became the head of public relations and marketing. One of the best things she did was a huge pig-roast weekend on the beach. It received national attention! We invited the best BBQ masters in the state of Florida, and they drove down to compete for a big cash prize. It was well-received within the hospitality industry.

Lucia even got Jon Bon Jovi to come perform at Penrod's on Miami Beach when he was about 18 years old. Bon Jovi was going to be in town promoting a band he was working with, the Great White , so Lucia reached out to his team and invited him to do a show. We worked with the city, the fire department, and the police department to ensure the safety and enjoyment of all concert-goers.

The one caveat we were given by the city was *not* to use Bon Jovi's name in marketing. So we'd advertise on radio stations and allude to having a "special, surprise guest" with "Wanted Dead or Alive" playing in the background. While we didn't say his name . . . people knew.

The event was a hit. The crowd stood elbow to elbow with a turn-out of about 5,000 people. Despite the concerns of the city, the event went off smoothly, with no issues at all.

When renowned promoter Judy Drucker brought Luciano Pavarotti to town to hold a concert on the sands of Miami Beach, the city asked us to assist by providing logistical support and food and beverage services. While we can't take credit for bringing in Pavarotti, we had quickly become Miami Beach's go-to partner for event support. Pavarotti's performance garnered national media coverage, further solidifying Miami Beach's emergence as a social and cultural epicenter.

Penrod's Miami Beach hosted countless events like these. We partnered with the Miami Beach Preservation League and helped them organize an Art Deco Weekend in celebration of Miami's art deco-influenced architecture. After paying my staff for their service, I always turned over any profits from these weekend events to the League. I genuinely just wanted to help make Miami Beach a better place for people to live and play.

Spring break in Miami Beach became profitable—although never to the level it had in Fort Lauderdale. We had to slow the acceleration down before it reached that point. But everything we touched down there was an opportunity to make money. When paper products were outlawed on the beach, I began selling plastic mugs with the name "Penrod's" emblazoned on them. I was making money in both Fort Lauderdale and Miami Beach. Things were going well.

But as things began to take off in Miami Beach, I had to manage the expectations of Bob Gill, my landlord at Sheraton Yankee Trader. He didn't want me to expand and threatened to lock me out of Penrod's Fort Lauderdale if I opened a full restaurant in Miami Beach. True to his word, on November 8, 1989, the day I opened Penrod's Miami Beach, Mr. Gill locked all my doors in Fort Lauderdale.

With things leveling off in Fort Lauderdale, I decided to find a new way to expand. In the mid 1980s, before Penrod's Miami Beach opened, I set my sights on Daytona Beach. I was back on top, and there was no reason to think I couldn't duplicate my success around the state. It was then that I began to lay the groundwork for my next successful venture.

In 1985, Daytona Beach made perfect sense for spring break. It was an easy drive for anyone in the Southeast. They also allowed driving on the beach—a marketing point that drew people from all over the world. A1A was wide and lined with stores, restaurants, and clubs. It was a logical place for me to promote. The city seemed excited about the possibilities of bringing more business to town. Plus, it would draw some of the crowd away from Fort Lauderdale, alleviating the congestion and inevitable debauchery that followed.

Excited about the prospects, I bought the largest hotel—the Carlton Plaza. It was a great beachfront property with a huge convention space. It had a huge pool deck, two existing bars, and 325 rooms. The bones of the hotel were terrific, but the property was in desperate need of renovation.

Learning from my previous mistakes, I hired a CPA firm and worked on a business plan. We ran the numbers and realized the investment was going to be astronomical. I partnered with a wealthy man: he put up the money, and I did the work. I quickly began a remodeling project. When students would book a room in my hotel, I'd ask them to pay an astronomical security deposit. That way, if they destroyed property, I'd have the ability to refurbish it without it coming out of my own pocket.

As the hotel took shape, I brainstormed ways to bring in the crowds. I had heard at the time that MTV was strapped for cash. The music network wasn't doing well, and they were looking for a new way to appeal to their youthful audience. I think I paid something like $35,000 to bring them to Daytona Beach. Their coverage of spring break was immensely popular—and it raised awareness for Daytona Beach.

Although the success was immediate, it was short-lived. MTV had no real loyalty—not to me, not to Daytona Beach. Though they came back out to Miami Beach for us, their participation in my marketing campaigns would only be for a short time; then they moved on to another spring-break hotspot. But the Daytona hotel was only busy for two months out of the year; the rest of the time, it sat vacant. I made the decision to sell before I lost too much money.

If there was one thing I learned from WUV's, it was the importance of cutting a business loose if it wasn't performing to my expectations. Previously, I would have hung on as long as humanly possible, hoping to think of a way to engage the other ten months. But if that turnaround never came, I could lose everything. I was willing to unload the Carlton Plaza as soon as it stopped being profitable. My quick thinking probably saved me from getting into another financial hole.

After selling the hotel, my business partner made the decision that he didn't want to be in the spring-break business anymore. And just like that, another decade-long adventure came to an end.

NIKKI BEACH

"I'm so lucky to be born who I was, because I don't need to think about tenacity. It's built into my DNA. I don't have to think about moving on after tragedy. It's built in too. Sometimes I may get off track or have a bad day, but I always come back to the core of who I am—a positive guy and a hard worker, just looking for my next adventure."

—JACK

Miami was no longer just a place for grandma and grandpa to go to retire. The average age of a citizen had dropped to under 40, and the city was thriving. But as I said, some of the same issues that plagued us in Fort Lauderdale began creeping into Miami Beach.

When the city asked me to slow it all down, I obliged. I never envisioned that my expansion into Miami Beach would be a short-term business or a seasonal, spring-break business. I had put my money where my mouth was to the tune of $4 million in building Penrod's Miami Beach. My intention there has always been longevity. It wasn't in my interest to upset neighbors and create chaos in a place where we were hoping to stay for 40-plus years. We wanted to build a strong, successful business with long-term goals. To this day, what's best for Miami Beach is what's best for us.

Before we shut down shop, we quit advertising for about four months to mitigate the influx of visitors to the beach. The strategy worked—the business went *way* down. So down, however, that we were losing money.

It felt like every city we set up in begged us to bring in the crowds, but once we did, they wanted those crowds to go back home. People wanted the impossible—the money of a thriving metropolis without any of the hassle. Another lesson I learned is that you can't please everybody, but you can do what's right.

I lost money for six years in Miami Beach because I was trying to be a good neighbor. I was thankful to have reserves, thanks to the ten good years at Penrod's Fort Lauderdale. But there was a lot of weight on my shoulders. I'd hired 500 employees for Penrod's Miami Beach because it had been such a big operation. I had a lot to keep up with. Unlike the Carlton Plaza in Daytona Beach, I didn't have a partner there to shoulder the cashflow demands. It was year nine before I even started breaking even at the Miami Beach Penrod's.

In the meantime, I was growing restless. My second divorce was underway, and I needed a new opportunity—a new adventure. In 1991, I was contacted by Edward Saint George who, along with Jack Hayward, held considerable interest in the city of Freeport in the Bahamas. Edward thought I could bring one of my projects (and my money) to Freeport, increasing the draw of tourists to the area. This venture was exactly what I needed at the time, so I picked up and moved to the Bahamas.

One of the projects I worked on most extensively is the area that is now known as Port Lucaya in Lucaya, a suburb of Freeport. During that time, I designed and planned a hotel that was much like the Penrod's Miami Beach. The boat slips in the marina increased by nearly ten times—moving from 12 to 100.

The views weren't bad in Freeport. I was given one of five houses on the beach to live in, and life was peaceful. But I missed my family. And I still had plenty of businesses in the States, so I moved back in 1994.

Things were changing in my personal life too. Lucia left Penrod's in 1990, and she and I became involved. I couldn't deny my attraction to her—not just because she is the most beautiful woman in the world, but because she is sharp, funny, and never lets me off the hook. I didn't want to get married again, but I didn't want to lose Lucia. In 1995, I made one of the very best decisions of my life and made Lucia a Penrod!

With my wife at my side, my thirst for adventure had never been stronger. Thankfully, Lucia already knew me well, and even helped get me out of a few tough situations. Take, for example, the time I got stranded on Moore's Island.

Out of all the toys I've ever owned—then or now—the seaplane is far and away my favorite. On one excursion I took by myself, I put the plane down so I could fish and eat. I wasn't even sure where I was. And when I got back in the plane, the engine wouldn't start.

I thought, *Well, the only way to get home is to swim.* I was 14 miles from the nearest island that had people on it. I got in the water and pulled my seaplane behind me. There were lots of sharks in this area, but I never really gave them a thought. I wasn't bothering them, so I figured they wouldn't bother me.

It took me until the next morning to swim and drag the seaplane that far, but once I reached the island—Moore's Island—I needed a new starter sent out. Only I didn't have any money. I wasn't planning on needing any!

Luckily, as I approached Moore's Island, someone saw me swimming inland, and they pulled me the rest of the way.

When I finally got to a phone and called Lucia, she was panicked. She had no idea what had become of me. I asked her to send some money so I could get a starter and get home. I got the part put in, and the plane started right up and I flew home.

That wasn't my only seaplane adventure either. Once, I landed near a reef and got out to fish again. But then, when I got on top of the plane to drop the anchor, the wind caught it and tossed me off. I was trying to hold on to the anchor when the cleat from the plane stuck right in my leg.

I was out there, all alone on a reef, with a cleat in my leg, bleeding like a stuffed pig. I took my T-shirt off and wrapped it around to stop the bleeding. It wasn't until the next day that I finally flew back home to get stitched up.

But it was on another trip in 1997 that my life changed forever.

I went to the Bahamas to go fishing. When I'm off the grid, I'm off the grid. No one can get in touch with me. When I got off the plane back in Miami, my daughter Tracey was there to meet me. She had tears pouring down her face.

"Dad," she sobbed, "it's Nikki."

Nicole was only 18 years old when the car she was a passenger in was hit by a drunk driver. She was two weeks away from high school graduation—14 days away from beginning the rest of her life.

I'm a strong man who has endured a lot. But in that moment, I collapsed on the tarmac, unable to process the idea of a world without my Nikki in it. One memory fell to the front of my mind.

"Dad?" she had recently asked. "Where do I stand when it comes to your kids? How do I fit in?"

"Well, Nikki," I responded easily, "you're the very best of my kids, and you're the very worst of my kids too."

Never had a truer description been given. Nicole had been a thrill seeker. She'd climb out bedroom windows, work the bar during spring break, and then she'd pick up a microphone at one of my clubs and start singing. She had a beautiful voice, and people were captivated by her. Me most of all.

I picked myself up off the concrete. I didn't know how I would move beyond this tragedy, but I also knew Nikki would have been disappointed if I'd allowed her passing to take the life out of me. I decided that instead of mourning her death, I was going to celebrate her life.

I went to the Miami Beach Penrod's location and immediately got to work, throwing myself into remodeling it into something worthy of my daughter's beauty, joy, and life. I wanted to re-create the place where she was born. When Nikki came into the world, I owned a boutique hotel called Café Martinique in Fort Lauderdale. It had a few rooms for rent and a beautiful garden and restaurant. When Nikki was born, everyone decorated the garden with pink balloons and signs saying "It's a Girl!"

So I started with the swimming pool. I filled it with fertilized soil, and I created the most lush, verdant garden—you would swear you were in a different country. We planted grown trees with orchids on them, colorful beds of flowers, and sumptuous greenery.

I personally planted all the trees in the garden. Well, I guess I had a little help—we had to use huge cranes to lift the trees from the parking lot over the building into what had been the pool area before I could dig them into the soil we'd hauled in.

My wife, Lucia, also created a butterfly garden on the second floor, because Nicole loved butterflies. There was a time when we had almost 200 cocoons. When they opened, the butterflies would fly down to the garden where we had food for them. At night, we'd light candles and tiny white twinkle lights glinted in the tree branches.

We did an opening and called the space Café Nikki, an homage to Café Martinique. But it wasn't a business opening. It was really an invitation for friends and family to come to enjoy nature and to remember Nikki—to celebrate life. Nicole's favorite flower was the sunflower, so at the entrance, I planted a Tabebuia tree. We hired a flower shop to create balls of sunflowers that hung from every branch of that tree. We also had a small fountain with the sound of running water.

It was magical.

I put Nicole's photograph up on the wall, and now millions of people have walked by and seen her beautiful face while connecting with the essence of Nicole's spirit—*life*. She had always been brimming with so much life.

"You should really go to therapy," someone suggested. But I'd always been able to work through my own problems. I'm not saying that's the case for everyone, but that's how I've always been. Nikki's garden was my therapy.

I would spend hours in that garden. It was both a refuge, full of peace, and an inspiration, vibrating with life and growth. Before I knew it, I wasn't the only one walking the garden of Café Nikki.

One day I was outside working on the flowers and I was approached by two surfers named Ted and Lindley. They told me they hosted an event for a bunch of young people called Beehive, up on Lincoln Road.

"There's surfers, models, wanna-be surfers, and wanna-be models there," they said. "We call it Beehive because we just want to be close with one another."

Looking at the garden, they liked what they saw. Their landlord had just raised the rent on the place they'd been meeting, and they asked if they could bring the Beehive to Café Nikki.

"No" was my immediate response. "This isn't a place for business."

I went home, and Lucia and I talked about it. I realized I'd been quick to respond, and I wasn't sure I'd made the right choice.

"What do you think Nikki would have wanted?" Lucia prompted.

At 18—the age Nikki was when she passed and around the age of these kids—she would have wanted a *party*.

I called Ted and Lindley. "Monday nights are yours," I told them.

Every Monday night, some of the most beautiful kids in Miami Beach gathered in Café Nikki with the butterflies, trees, and white lights, just to be close to one another. I can't imagine a more fitting way to honor Nicole.

All of a sudden, Café Nikki was the place to be. Leonardo DiCaprio was about 18 years old when he came through, wearing his little round glasses. Madonna, Harrison Ford, and Michael Douglas visited as well—celebrities from all over flocked to that location. I realized that what had become an outlet for my grief was also a place for others to celebrate life.

At the time, Miami was offering incentives to the modeling and movie industries to come film in the city, so there was no shortage of celebrities in the area. And they all wanted to be in Nikki's place. So we decided to expand. We never had plans for Café Nikki to become a huge business, but the customers created a demand. I was happy people enjoyed the space as much as I did.

In July 1997, Lucia and I went to the South of France. While there, we visited a few beach clubs. These types of clubs had been in business across the Mediterranean for decades. I came back with amazing ideas about the vibes of these successful businesses and how to run them. I felt confident that I could come up with a unique concept that would honor the young life of Nicole.

In 1998, we expanded onto the beach area and Nikki Beach Miami Beach was born. I wanted this concept to be personal—we were honoring my daughter. We wanted to create a beach club that was warm and welcoming for friends and family to enjoy.

When I was a little boy, my mom (who was adopted) used to tell me stories about Native American tribes. As a kid, I loved this. We wanted to incorporate that part of my childhood into Nikki Beach Miami Beach. With the help of a designer, we came up with the idea to put teepees on the beach. We outfitted the entire place, including the staff, in all white. "You're crazy," people said. "All white on the *beach*?"

I didn't care. To me, it looked like heaven.

There were no sharp edges in the design plan. We hung free-flowing curtains everywhere. All aspects of the aesthetic were soft, feminine, and safe. Our tables were made from natural wood of non-endangered species of trees that I personally sourced from Vietnam. I've always believed in the flow of energy, so it was very important to me to make sure that people felt good the moment they walked into the space. Everything had movement.

Nikki Beach was met with instant success. Four-hour lunches with rosé and Champagne were unheard of in the United States. But clients held them daily at Nikki Beach. We invited a well-traveled DJ to play music for our guests. He brought in a unique mix of chill music that paired perfectly with wine and lunch. The genre was so different that people used to hear songs on the radio and say, "That sounds like Nikki Beach!"

We wanted the safe, laidback, protected feel of family and friends, so we didn't want to blare our names across the radio for advertisement. We wanted controlled traffic to maintain the laidback, casual atmosphere that allowed so many people to simply savor the moment. We wanted our guests' stay to be a Celebration of Life—which has become a cornerstone of the Nikki Beach brand.

We're not looking for *any* guest; we're looking for the *right* guest. That's why the marketing strategy has always been our motto "Tell Only Your Best Friends." We'd tell our clients on their way out, "Come back. Oh, but tell *only* your best friends about us." Not "tell a friend," but tell *only* your best friends—the people in your life like you. "Tell Only Your Best Friends" has been my most effective marketing strategy to date.

Along with our guests, we want our staff to feel as if they're among family and friends too. You can't buy loyalty from employees—you have to earn it. Like I did back in my McDonald's days, I have taken the time to intentionally invest in my staff. We put in the work to make sure each employee feels a sense of belonging, meaning, and connection.

I have seen many of the staff grow up. I have watched them get married and have children. I've been honored to witness their becoming. We've shared stories—the good and the bad—which is what family really is all about.

And the brand values come through these relationships—the philosophy and the service. Our "welcome home" environment is transmitted from the top down, so when people come to the brand, they feel a connection and have an emotional experience.

Even though family has always been so important to me, the family our brand has developed feels more like a biological family than I could have ever dreamed of. Their commitment to what we've built together translates to the experience of the guests across countries and cultures. Our staff is essential to the magic of the Nikki Beach brand.

I'm so grateful and humbled that life gave me my extended Nikki Beach family.

Speaking of family—on November 26, 2001, I started my next great adventure. Lucia gave birth to our twins, Jake and Isabella! Our Saint Tropez location would open the next year, and I had made some big changes to the beach club. I took out the parking lot, expanded the pool, and did extensive renovations all around. With all the traveling back and forth, I knew I didn't want to miss out on time with my newborns. I decided to take them and Lucia with me.

We stayed together in a villa in Saint Tropez for two months every summer. I was able to keep a close eye on how things were running and being managed, all while juggling two growing babies in a foreign country. Those are some of my best memories—I even got to teach the twins how to swim there! I was in my mid sixties, but I felt younger and more alive than ever.

Just after we opened in 2002, Naomi Campbell reached out and asked if we would host her birthday party.

"Sure," I said. "What do you have in mind?"

Her boyfriend at the time owned Cirque du Soleil, and he was footing the bill. "The sky is the limit," we were told.

So to the sky we reached. Naomi wanted her soiree to be an all-white party. By the time of the event, there wasn't a stitch of white clothing left at any of the local boutiques—it had all been snatched up by the over 1,000-person guest list she insisted on having.

It was incredible that the first party that Nikki Beach Saint Tropez threw was for one of the world's top models, enjoying our brand with 1,000 of her closest friends. That made us look pretty darn good—especially in those early days when Nikki Beach was in its infancy. That was over 20 years ago, and we've only continued to grow.

While I was in Saint Tropez one summer, several years after opening, Lucia and I sat at the table of the owner of the Orient Express. He turned to me and said, "Jack, how does it feel to know that you changed the way that people party around the world?"

I looked at Lucia, not sure what the man meant.

"You created a daytime party concept," the man continued, "where people are dancing and enjoying drinks and food, but it's all done in a healthy environment."

I realized the man was right. But I had been in the trenches for so long that I never really saw it that way before. In that moment, I felt a great sense of pride. I was proud of our team, our brand, and our name.

On the heels of such amazing success, my wife and I had one of the scariest moments of our lives. Our daughter Isabella ended up in the hospital in Nice, France, where she was diagnosed with a rare genetic condition called tuberous sclerosis. We flew back to the U.S. immediately and went to the head of neurology at Miami Children's Hospital for a second opinion.

I always thought my twins were born with a lucky star because a friend of mine, Jim Clark, founder of Netscape, offered us his G5 to make the trip from France back home. "I don't want you to have to stop," he told us. "Take my plane so you can go straight to Miami."

I'm so grateful for his generosity.

The head of the neurology department confirmed Isabella's diagnosis. They also told us that since Isabella was so young, six months old, they couldn't guarantee how the condition would affect her life. She may not be able to walk or talk, or she may be a completely typical child. It was a difficult time for both Lucia and me.

Over the next months, while Lucia took Isabella to specialists from all over, I spent time with my boy Jake. One day I walked into the living room and he had all the cushions piled up.

"What are you doing, Jake?"

He said, "Oh, I just invented a money machine." Jake had put piles of quarters on top of the cushions and they were cascading down. He thought he was making money.

"That's my boy," I said.

With the amazing reputation that we had established with two Nikki Beach locations, representatives started reaching out, expressing a desire for us to bring our brand to their countries.

I got a call to come to a lunch with Michael Douglas, Catherine Zeta-Jones, and the governor of Bermuda. "I want a Nikki Beach in Bermuda," the governor told me. I had to politely decline because, at the time, Bermuda was not my ideal market. I might revisit that decision, but I don't regret saying no when I did.

When I lived in New York with the Rockefellers, they used to take me to Sardis, a famous restaurant that had pictures on the wall of all the celebrity guests who had dined there. People would go there and see Frank Sinatra, Marilyn Monroe, Gary Cooper, and Grace Kelly.

When I went to France, they do a thing called the Cannes Film Festival. I said, "I'm going to do the same thing Sardis did. Celebrities love our spot so much, that's really all the marketing I need."

I set up a temporary location—a pop-up, they call them—and we opened for ten days during the international film festival in Cannes. I got Champagne companies to sponsor the event, so we had the best bubbly flowing freely for anyone who attended. Every celebrity in the industry has come through our Cannes Nikki Beach pop-up over the years. We have pictures of Nicole Kidman, Bruce Willis, Colin Farrell, Keith Urban, Robert Pattinson, Javier Bardem, Jake Gyllenhaal, Ben Stiller, Tilda Swinton, Adam Sandler, and Denzel Washington. In fact, we have had so many celebrities come through that I once created a Nikki Beach magazine just to publish all of them.

After the success of the pop-up at the Cannes International Film Festival, and over the years, we did pop-ups at the Toronto Film Festival, the Venice Film Festival, and the Sundance Film Festival. We became the home away from home for all of Hollywood.

The same year we opened Saint Tropez (2002), we also opened Nikki Beach Saint Barth. In 2003, we expanded to Spain and Italy. And we're still growing.

I own a farm in North Carolina, and once in a while, I like to remember my teenage years in Homestead, where I learned how to drive a tractor. One day I took out my own state-of-the-art Bace, I got on it, and I started playing around in the woods. Out in nature, my first love, I started thinking: the beach club business is a phenomenal business, but it requires a lot of attention and care to maintain at an excellent level. To leave a sustainable legacy to my family, I needed to find something that could survive me. I thought about how much more stable the hotel business was. I knew that putting a Nikki Beach at a hotel would create more security and continuity.

Up until this point, none of my Nikki Beach locations had hotels. I decided to make a massive move by opening a new luxury hotel under the same name in Koh Samui, Thailand. Our reputation in the hospitality industry was so well-respected that I got a call from the Sheikh of Dubai to request a meeting with me.

He went to shake my hand and said, "Jack Penrod?"

"Yes, sir," I replied.

He said he was honored to meet me and that he would love for me to bring my brand to Dubai. After the opening there, investors started approaching me from left and right. "You should put a Nikki Beach in this country and this country," they said.

Today, we have hotels and resorts in locations like Thailand, Greece, Montenegro, Dubai, and Oman.

One question I often get asked is why Nikki Beach has become so successful. I believe it's because Nikki Beach's growth was completely organic. It was the combination of a lot of my business and life philosophies:

- Listen to your customers and give them more of what they want.
- Don't have a brand that customers need to be educated on.
- Your music, your food, and your aesthetic are all products.

The result is that Nikki Beach feels like home to those who visit.

We cater to a discerning customer who can afford anything they want. The fact that they come to us is a testament to our friendly service, premium quality, and that we aren't trying to impress anyone. We demonstrate the DNA of our humility by serving their needs and wants before they ask for either. We give them a stage to shine on and make them look good in front of their friends and family.

There are countless details that are involved in running our business, so we created six elements that serve as our pillars of marketing: music, dining, entertainment, fashion, film, and art. We make sure that every day we are open, at every location, we convey these elements to create a seamless brand experience—the magic of Nikki Beach.

Nikki Beach is unlike anything I've ever done in my career. It's more fulfilling than anything I've ever done too. But even Nikki Beach hasn't slowed my penchant for the adrenaline of adventure.

In 2012, my next-door neighbor, a Navy Seal from Israel, introduced me to a beautiful diving area on the far side of Cuba. Because American aircrafts could not fly direct to Cuba, we flew my plane to Cancun, and from Cancun we flew into Cuba.

We met up with the diving company and drove for four hours across the country to meet a boat. Then it was a three-hour boat ride to our dive location. The idea was to wear a scuba tank and observe the sharks. At our first dive, there was a beautiful area where the sharks were everywhere—maybe a hundred of them. It was wonderful.

We took a break back on the boat to get new tanks and have a bit of a rest. During that time, there were other boats nearby, and one of them was observing these giant rats on the island—they were as big as dogs! I can't say I was dying to see them for myself, but it was fascinating to me that a creature like that even existed.

Then it was time for our second dive. I got in the water and noticed this Goliath-sized grouper just hanging around. He was probably six feet long and weighed around 500 pounds. I decided to leave the grouper be, and I turned my attention back to the sharks.

The next thing I knew, something tapped me on the back. When I turned around, that giant grouper grabbed my hand with his mouth and would not let go. One of my buddies in the dive noticed the problem and helped me pull my hand out. I hadn't been wearing a glove, so my hand got fairly mangled. I had to get out of the water immediately, because a bleeding hand brings on a multitude of sharks.

I got in the boat and I knew I had to do some kind of infection prevention. The guy who had been observing the dog-sized rats on the island had mentioned that one of the women in their group was a veterinarian. Remembering this, we called on the radio and got her to come to the boat. Miraculously, she had a special medicine that prevented infection from fish injuries.

I soaked my hand in the solution before she wrapped it up. Then I took a small boat back to the mainland and grabbed a cab to take me to Havana. The driver was in no hurry—he stopped on the way to the hospital and ate at somebody's house while I waited in the cab. As soon as I had a cellphone signal, I called Lucia.

"You've got to get me out of Cuba," I told her.

"Jack," she said, "it's not like I can Google 'How to get an American out of Cuba.' You're not supposed to be there!"

I'll never hear the end of that one. See, while our entrance into Cuba may have been creative, it hadn't been strictly legal.

Luckily, my son Mike was staying at our house that day, and he knew a hotel operator in Havana, so I had a room for the night. The next day I flew from Havana to Cancun, and Lucia arranged for our pilot to get me from Cancun back to Miami.

My doctor was waiting for me at the emergency room at Mount Sinai on Miami Beach. He was concerned about me developing an infection, since 24 hours had passed since I'd been bitten. There were two other doctors in the emergency room who were ex-Marines and thought it was so funny I'd been bitten by a grouper. They looked at it, they checked the medicine that I took for the infection, and they said it was all good.

They cleaned it, wrapped it up, and sent me home.

By the way, that grouper left me with a souvenir—I can still feel a tooth under my skin. Since I've shot so many groupers during my hunting trips in the Keys and the Bahamas, I figure that big ol' guy was just getting even with me.

There's no amount of success or money that could curb my love for adventure and the great outdoors. In fact, I bet people would be surprised by how little I would personally require to be happy in life. People meet me and they say, "How did you go from being a hamburger man to being the owner of a luxury brand like Nikki Beach?"

The truth is, there isn't much difference between what I'm offering either guest—a McDonald's guest or a Nikki Beach guest. Lucia always teases me that my spring-break customers have now grown up and moved on from beer to Champagne. Maybe she's right. I like that idea very much.

The truth is that people just want to enjoy their lives, enjoy each other, and enjoy good food in an environment that fits their lifestyle.

By the way, I'll never be too "high-class" for a decent burger. There's still a lot of hamburger man left in me. In business, whatever you do, you have to stay true to yourself. People sense phony efforts—at least over time.

As for Nikki Beach? Nikki Beach was built on the truest experiences I've ever had—the experiences of love and family.

EPILOGUE ADVENTURING ON

"Persistence is optimism and hard work."
—JACK

My entire life, my family has always been the most important investment I've made. I had twins at the age of 64—when my first three children were already grown. In fact, most of my *grandkids* are older than my twins! Regardless of the broken marriages, my kids have come first in everything.

Nikki Beach wouldn't be my last adventure—not by a long shot. But I take life a bit more seriously now. At 83 years old, I've never had more to live for.

I wake up every morning and I walk a few miles in the warm Florida sunshine. Then I go and lift something heavy to build up my muscle tone. I end my hour-and-a-half workout sessions with a stint in the sauna. I'm hoping to sweat out the mercury in my system that I'm told I have too much of.

Nikki Beach is as successful as any brand I've been a part of. I'm immensely proud of our name, our product, and our reputation.

With all of my experiences, all of my adventures, and all of my successes, if anyone asks me where I feel the most peace and happiness, it's when I'm spending time in the Bahamas with my children, grandchildren, and great-grandchildren—and especially my wife, Lucia. I am biased, but she is brilliant.

I have five incredible children—Michelle, Tracey, Michael, Jake, and Isabella. I'm very proud of the adults they've all grown up to be. With her persistence, tenacity, and hard work, Isabella has exceeded all expectations and is doing well in college. I see myself in my son Jake and how he handles challenges. He has tackled some detours that could have been catastrophic. Just as all teenage boys do, he's learned from his mistakes. He's a survivor—just like me. He's extremely creative and is pursuing a music career. I can see his determination and total conviction. He has no self-doubt, which is saying a lot for a 20-something in today's world.

As for my older children, they have what I have always wished most for them—beautiful, loving families. When we all get together, our immediate family is made up of 16 people. I've been able to see the lives they have built for themselves. They have children and grandchildren running around, laughing and playing.

What more can a man ask for?

Chronologically, I may be 83 years old, but some tests I had run recently say that my biological age is 61. Emotionally, some days I feel like an old man, but mostly I feel like that 10-year-old boy arriving in Homestead, full of ideas, plans, and potential.

And my mind hasn't slowed down a bit. I may vacation a little more than I used to, but I'll always be the same hamburger man, strategizing and innovating until it's my time to go. Why? Because I consistently crave new challenges.

When I tell people my story, that's what I get asked about—the challenges. "Jack, how did you make it? How did you overcome all the challenges you faced?"

I guess one of the ways I've always been lucky is in my perspective. Because when I look back on my life, I really don't see that many *challenges*. Obstacles, maybe. Delays. But really, challenges are just adventures that choose us instead of us choosing them.

The Great Depression, poverty, being raised by a single mom, enduring an abusive stepdad, a few failed relationships, bankruptcy, and some scrapes and stitches may seem like setbacks to some. But for me, life has been one grand adventure. And as long as I am breathing on this earth, I'll adventure on until the very end.

I've lived a good life, but I'm not done yet. I still have deals to make, trips to take, and children, grandchildren, and great-grandchildren to invest in. I hope that when I do make my last dollar, and I'm laid in the ground, my loved ones do not grieve for me. I've made friends, made money, and made *life*.

Life is, after all, whatever you make of it.

ACKNOWLEDGEMENTS

First and foremost, I'd like to thank my beautiful and brilliant wife Lucia for urging me to share my adventures with the world. Without her hard work, encouragement, and love, I can assure you this book would have never seen the light of day.

Thank you to my kids, Michele, Tracey, Michael, Jake and Isabella. Thank you for teaching me what it means to be a father. I learn from you all every day, and I hope you learn from me as well. I mean it when I say you will always be my greatest adventure.

To all of our Nikki Beach staff, thank you for executing our vision and strategy to give people a place to come home to. It's easy to write a book about an incredible brand. It's much more difficult to create that brand. But you show up every day, ready to work hard and show people a good time.

And finally, I have to express gratitude to Nicole—the muse of Nikki Beach. It is your magic, charisma, and love for life that inspired a brand that has changed and enhanced the lives of countless people. May you always be remembered as full of life, laughter, and joy.

My father, Vernon Penrod in his 20's.

Grandma Townsend (far left) watching over us and a handful of relatives.

Chuck (my brother) and I shooting marbles in Columbus, Ohio (with little sister, Carol Ann watching).

Chuck (brother) and I in the backyard of Grandma Townsend's home in Columbus, Ohio.

My mother.

On the stairs of Grandma Townsend's home in Columbus, Ohio. Chuck (brother), Bob (brother), me, Carol Ann (sister) and our neighbor, Roberta Solomon and her brother.

Mom, Chuck (brother), me, Carol Ann (sister)
and Bob (brother) in Columbus, Ohio.

Mom in the early 1940's.

My first dog, Skip.

My beautiful mother.

Chuck (brother) and I with our
Salvation Army coats.

Chuck (brother), Carol Ann (sister) and me.

From left, Vernon (dad), Chuck (brother) me, Carol Ann (sister) and Bob (brother) in Columbus, Ohio when I was almost 8 years old. My mom was the photographer.

Chuck, me, Tommy Royal, Ruben Mills and a friend in the Florida Keys.

My senior year portrait.

Playing with my camera in New York.

After working my first year in the keys, I bought this beautiful car - paid for in cash.

Marine Corps, 1962.

THIS M-FOSTER—"CANYON RUNNER"—WAS ON MAIDEN VOYAGE
where Jack Penrod of Fort Lauderdale and went from Mariposa off Cuba

One of my first boats during my early
20's, a 25' Betram.

In celebration of the opening of their fifteenth
McDonald's Restaurant
Jack, Bob and Chuck Penrod
invite you to join them for wine and cheese
Wednesday, March 13, 1974 from 5 — 7 P.M. at the newest
McDonald's
5511 West Oakland Park Blvd.
Lauderhill, Florida
Guest of honor for the evening is
Ray Kroc,
Founder and Chairman of the Board of McDonald's.
R.S.V.P. 522-1848 or 527-0076

My 31' Allied Seawind Catch, named
Island Girl, in the Florida Keys.

One of my McDonald's locations.

Carol Ann (sister), Mary (sister-in-law) and myself in
front of my McDonald's in Davie, FL in the late 1960's.

A typical night of Mom and the boys.

Penrod's on Ft. Lauderdale Beach, FL.

Mom and her three boys.

Mom and I at one of her weddings.

My spearfishing days with my seaplane
in the Bahamas.

Lee Lacocca, a friend, and my brother-in-law,
Alan Paulson.